Java and C

COMPUTER PROGRAMMING FOR BEGINNERS

2 BOOK IN ONE

A practical beginners guide to learn java and C programming, fundamentals and code

Will Norton

Text Copyright © [Bill Norton]

Legal & Disclaimer

The information contained in this book and its contents is not designed to replace or take the place of any form of medical or professional advice; and is not meant to replace the need for independent medical, financial, legal or other professional advice or services, as may be required. The content and information in this book has been provided for educational and entertainment purposes only.

The content and information contained in this book has been compiled from sources deemed reliable, and it is accurate to the best of the Author's knowledge, information and belief. However, the Author cannot guarantee its accuracy and validity and cannot be held liable for any errors and/or omissions. Further, changes are periodically made to this book as and when needed. Where appropriate and/or necessary, you must consult a professional (including but not limited to your doctor, attorney, financial advisor or such other professional advisor) before using any of the suggested remedies, techniques, or information in this book.

Upon using the contents and information contained in this book, you agree to hold harmless the Author from and against any damages, costs, and expenses, including any legal fees potentially resulting from the application of any of the information provided by this book. This disclaimer applies to any loss, damages or injury caused by the use and application, whether directly or indirectly, of any advice or information presented, whether for breach of contract, tort, negligence, personal injury, criminal intent, or under any other cause of action.

You agree to accept all risks of using the information presented inside this book.

You agree that by continuing to read this book, where appropriate and/or necessary, you shall consult a professional (including but not limited to your doctor, attorney, or financial advisor or such other advisor as needed) before using any of the suggested remedies, techniques, or information in this book.

Table of Contents

INTRODUCTION

The history of Java dates back to 1991 when programmers Patrick Haughton, Mike Sheridan, and James Gosling thought of a programming language that could best be used for the development of Digital TV. However, it was deemed to be way ahead of its own time, and thus, they redeveloped it based on the C+ and C++ platforms to make it easier and more economical to use.

With the redevelopment also came the core principles of Java, which are:

It has to be portable—or that it should work on as many platforms as possible, without any of them not working as well as the other;

It should be safe and secure to use—and definitely well encrypted;

People should feel connected to it in as little time as possible, which means that they should be working with words that are somehow familiar to them, and even though it looks complex at first, sooner or later, they have to realize that it actually works;

It should be dynamic, should work in threads, and could be modified when needed, and;

It should perform with precision.

As you can see, these core principles give you the feeling that the programmers real made Java for the people—so they can enjoy using more programs without having to buy too many devices.

In 1995, Sun Microsystems finally released Java 1.0—the first public inception of Java, which had amazing security, no-cost runtimes, and file access restrictions across all networks. Over the years, 7 more Java releases had been made, and ever since 2006, Java started to be available through GNU, or General Public License—meaning it is now a free, open-source programming language. This stemmed from the public outcry that happened once when some of its contents were made private and only available for a fee, which definitely does not resonate with its core principles.

Start reading this book now and you'll learn more about Java in no time!

Chapter 1: What is Java?

Java is a programming language that is built by Sun Microsystems, which was later taken over by the Oracle Corporation. It is designed to run on any operating system that supports Java. This is what made the language so popular, because the developer just had to write the program once, and the program could then run on any operating system without the need for the programmer to change the code.

Most of the modern applications built around the world are made from the Java programming language. Most of the server side and business logic components of major applications are built on the Java programming language.

During the entire course of this book you will learn how to write programs such as the one above, and also learn advanced concepts that will enable you to start writing complete application programs.

Some of the design goals for Java are mentioned below:

- The language is intended to be written once and have the ability to be run on any operating system.

- The language should provide support for numerous software engineering principles.

- The language is intended to be used in developing software components suitable for deployment in distributed environments.

Portability is an important factor. This is why Java has the ability to run on Windows, Linux and the MacOS operating system.

Support for internationalization is very important.

Java is intended to be suitable for writing applications for both hosted and embedded systems.

Other design goals are discussed next:

1.1 Strong Type Checking

Java is a strong type language. Every variable that is defined needs to be attached to a data type.

You don't need to understand the complete program for now, but let's just have a quick look at 2 lines of the code.

1) int i=5;

Here we are defining something known as a variable, which is used to hold a value. The value that can be stored depends on the data type. In this example we are saying that 'i' is of the type 'int' or Integer, which is a number data value.

Array Bounds Checking

At runtime, Java will check whether the array has the required number of values defined. If one tries to access a value which is outside the bounds of the array, an exception will be thrown.

You don't need to understand the complete program for now, but let's just have a quick look at the following lines of the code.

1) int[] array1 = new int[2];

Here we are declaring an array, which is a set of integer values. The value of '2' means that we can only store two values in the array.

2) array1[0] = 1;

```
array1[1] = 2;
array1[2] = 3;
```

With this code we can see that we are assigning 3 values to the array. When you run this program, you will get an error because the program will see that the array has gone out of its maximum allowable bounds of two. You will get the below error at runtime.

```
Exception in thread "main"
java.lang.ArrayIndexOutOfBoundsException: 2
```

at HelloWorld.main(HelloWorld.java:8)

Chapter 2: Why Java is important?

Next, Java has syntax and features that resemble other programming languages like C and C++. If you have any prior programming experience, you will find learning Java a breeze. Even if you are totally new to programming, you can rest assured that Java is designed to be a relatively easy language to learn. Most programmers find it easier to learn Java than say, C or C++.

Java is also designed to be platform independent. As mentioned earlier, Java code is compiled into bytecode first, which can be run on any machine that has the Java Virtual Machine.

Hence with Java, you can write the code once and run it anywhere you want.

Next, Java is an object-oriented programming (OOP) language. Object-oriented programming is an approach to programming that breaks a programming problem into objects that interact with each other.

We'll be looking at various object-oriented programming concepts in this book. Once you master Java, you will be familiar with these concepts. This will make it easier for you to master other object-oriented programming languages in future.

Basic Tips

How has java become so successful? Java is such a widespread language for many reasons, and it owes a lot around the key principles it was designed around. One of the first principles of Java is its ease of use.

The fundamentals of the Java programming language were adapted from C ++, another extremely popular higher – level programming language.

However, though C ++ and its predecessors, C and C # are powerful languages, it tends to be rather complex in terms of syntax, and is not fully adapted for some of the purposes of Java, notably for internet technology integration.

Java thus was able to base itself on C ++, and build on this powerful language's fundamentals in order to provide a language that is also similarly powerful, but easier to use and better – suited for some specialized users.

Java is also a very reliable programming language, intentionally build in order to reduce and even eliminate the possibilities of fatal errors that arise from programmer errors. This is why Java heavily relies on object – oriented programming principles, which allows the data and the manipulation of data to be packaged together, making Java more robust and reliable, as well as much more modular, allowing for code packages to be switched out and adapted as needed.

In addition to the previous qualities of ease of use and reliability, given Java's nature of initially being designed for mobile devices, it was designed to be able to provide a higher level of security and safety for its programming, as it was initially meant for mobile devices, which by their nature are meant to exchange data over networks, making data security of the utmost priority.

Due to this, Java has become one of the most secure programming languages widely available today, making it a highly attractive option to those who wish to write programs that are less vulnerable to exploits.

Also, though Java was initially intended for mobile devices, Java has developed into a relatively platform – independent programming language, something that works to its advantage, as programs written in Java tend to work no matter what machine is running the program.

Java was written as a language that would be portable and work cross – platform, meaning that it doesn't matter what operating system the machine has, what hardware the machine is running, or what device it's running on.

This has led to its adaptability and its widespread use around the world. Due to these core principles prioritized by the Sun Microsystems team that developed Java: Ease of Use, Reliability, Safety, Cross – platform adaptability, Java became and still remains one of the most popular and most widely used programming languages today.

Why Java?

Of course, one of the key reasons to use Java is its focus on Object – oriented programming.

Object – oriented programming, or "OOP" is a type of programming language model which allows the program's code to be organized around data, rather than functions and logic, which is known as procedural programming.

These "data clusters" are organized into things called "objects", hence the moniker of "object – oriented programming".

These objects are created by something called "classes", understood here in the traditional sense of how classes are: types of objects, allowing the programmer to "classify" them according to two major criteria: attributes and methods.

The attributes of a class are the raw data that will create the object: these are its descriptors, such as the values that it possesses, and other relevant data that will make up the object. The second criterion is the "method" of the object.

This "method" is the behavior, or the logical sequences contained within the class, describing how it interacts or can be interacted with natively.

Chapter 3: Basics of Java

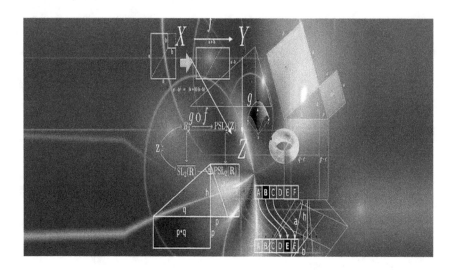

Java tokens

Java tokens are the values that are smaller than other integers.

These numbers are going to fall between the value of -32768 and 32767. The code that I have been using is not going to work for shorts, instead I am going to need to use the short function so that I can make sure that the values are going to fall between the set limitations.

Large values are going to be stored inside of a double value along with floating point values.

A double does not have to be used if I can use a floating point.

As I am storing a floating variable. I am going to need to put a letter at the end of my value amount. This value should be f because it is a floating point number.

Keywords

In Java, the Boolean type refers to false or true values. Java finds out if it is true or false using the reserved keywords. Therefore, an expression Boolean type will assume one of these values. An example to demonstrate include:

There are a few things to note about this program.

First, the **println()**, displays a boolean value.

Secondly, the boolean values control the flow of an if statement.

You don't need to go the long way in writing the boolean type this way: **if (b == true)**

The result shown by the operator such as < is boolean.

It is one of the reasons why we have the expression **11 > 8** showing the value **true**.

In addition, the other pair of parentheses near the **11 > 8** is important since plus comes before the >.

Identifiers

The top layer of the diagram above is for the identifier or name. This top layer is the name you give to a class.

The name should specifically identify and also describe the type of object as seen or experienced by the user.

In simple terms, the name or identifier should identify the class.

Operators

Java has an extensive list of operator environment.

If you are wondering what an operator is, you can look at it as a symbol which conveys a specific message to the compiler to carry out a logical or mathematical operation. I

n Java, you will interact with four classes of operators.

The four classes include:

- **Logical operator**

- **Bitwise operator**

- **Relational operator**

- **Arithmetic operator**

Like other computer languages, Java has a defined list of additional operators to take care of certain specific scenarios.

When it comes to learning JAVA programming language, or any programming language for that matter, there are five basic concepts you must understand before you get started.

These five basic concepts include:

1. **Variables**

2. **Data Structures**

3. **Control Structures**

4. **Syntax**

5. **Tools**

Each of these concepts will be thoroughly explained on a beginner's level to ensure that they are understood.

Separators

They are not suitable for high-level abstraction: note that a lot of these programs make use of low-level constructs which are primarily used for low-level abstraction.

The usual approach with these programming languages is that they focus on the machine – how to make a computer do something rather than how these functions can help solve the issues of a user.

These languages deal with the minute details, which is already beyond the scope of high-level abstraction, which is the more common approach that we see today.

In low-level abstraction, data structures and algorithms are taken separately whereas these are taken as a whole in high-level abstraction.

Literals

When it comes to literals in Java, we mean the fixed values which appear in the form in which human beings can read. We can say the number 200 is a literal.

Most of the time, literals can be constants.

Literals are important in a program. In fact, most Java programs use literals. Some of the programs we have already discussed in this book use literals.

Literals in Java can fall on various primitive data types.

The manner in which every literal is shown is determined by its type. Like it was mentioned some time back, we enclose character constants in single quotes such as **'c'** and **'%'**.

We define literals in integers without involving the fractional part.

For instance, 12 and -30 are integer literals.

A floating point literal should contain the decimal point plus the fractional part. 12.389 is a floating literal.

Java further permits for one to apply the scientific notation for the floating point literals.

Integer literals contain int value and anyone can initialize them with a variable of **short**, **byte,** and **char**.

comments

When this occurs, we call the grey's comments.

In the running stages of the program, the grey's (comments) are moot.

This is to mean that you can use the comment feature to state or explain what the code you are creating wants to achieve.

You can achieve this by typing two slashes and then the comment.

Here is a sample.

//Place your single line comment here

You can have more than one comment line by doing either of the following:

//We are going to

//spread the comments into two

Or

/*
This comment spreads over two lines

*/

If you look at the comment above, you will notice that it starts with /* but ends with */

Additionally, if you look at the previous image (figure 8) you will notice that there are comments that begin with a single forward slash and two asterisks (/**) but end with one asterisks and one forwards slash; this is called a Javadoc comment.

Chapter 4: What is Java Virtual Machine?

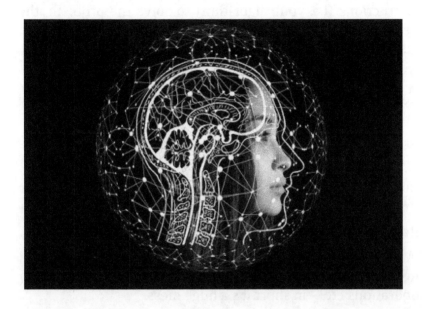

A virtual machine is software that emulates a physical machine. In traditional programming languages, code is compiled into machine language for a specific platform.

In Java, code is compiled into a virtual machine language called bytecode.

The JVM acts as an intermediary between bytecode and the underlying physical machine.

Every platform that supports Java has its own implementation of the JVM.

Java applications are portable because every JVM adheres to a standard interface.

The distribution package of the JVM and standard libraries is called the Java Runtime Environment (JRE).

The distribution package of the JRE and development tools, such as the compiler and debugger, is called the Java Development Kit (JDK).

Going back to the initial problem that we introduced earlier (i.e. making a compute radd 1 + 1), now we have a set of instructions (i.e. your algorithm) to solve the problem, the next thing you need to do is to translate that into instructions that a computer can understand.

Remember that a computer doesn't speak English or any other human language.

As it was explained earlier, you need to translate all those instructions to a series of binary signals.

But doing all that translation work will take up a lot of your time.

Remember that each character is composed of at least 8 bits.

After that you need to string them up into actual instructions to access computer memory and then do a math operations etc.—in short it's a huge mess.

No one wants to deal with that.

So, you speak a different language and the computer speaks a different one.

Well, how are you going to get both parties to meet halfway?

That is where programming languages like Java come in.

Think of a programming language as a go-between language that both computers and also human beings can understand—well so to speak, we'll clarify the details behind that in a little bit.

The goal here is to make the computer understand your instructions.

There are two phases that will happen before you can accomplish that.

The first step is to write your algorithm using a programming language. Yes, a go between language between you and the machine.

Well, computers still can't completely understand all the stuff that you will write even though it is already in Java code. And that is where step 2 comes in (2 steps remember?)—your Java code will then be processed by a program called a compiler.

As it was explained earlier when we covered the components of the Java platform, a compiler is a program or app that translates your programming code into machine readable instructions (aka instructions that your computer can understand).

There are actually a few more things that will happen in the background like a pre-compiling step as well as accessing Java libraries (mentioned earlier), then there is the actual translation into binary codes via an assembler, and more lines of code added to your original code that you wrote.

Again, all of that happens in the background.

As a Java programmer you shouldn't worry about that because the Java platform was developed to handle all of that.

It's fun to know and maybe when your programming skills have leveled up then you can go into the low level programming details yourself.

Now there is one last bit of preliminary info that you should know about before we can dive right into writing your Java programming code. And that is the Java Virtual Machine.

There is a recurring problem about the different types of hardware and software that are available in different devices today.

The hardware and software components of a smart phone will behave differently compared to that of your car or maybe your laptop.

To make things more complicated, the combination of different processor chips, different operating systems, and different arrays of electrical components will mean different ways to compile (or translate) the code you have written.

You need to make machine code specific to the platform of the device that you are programming.

So, what is the Java Virtual Machine or JVM?

It is a program or application that is designed to run computer programs on any device or machine.

It was quite a revolutionary program when it was released in 1995 and it is still a huge innovation today.

It solved the dilemma that was described earlier.

Think of the JVM as a kind of virtual computer inside your computer. It actually has two main functions.

The first one is to run any program on any device and on any operating system or software.

This is summarized in the principle of "write once, run anywhere" – you'll hear that a lot and other programming rules of thumb as you gain more experience. T

he other function is allocating memory space—and it is very good at managing a computer's memory.

The JVM is loaded on a computer's memory (RAM). It is independent, which means it can run on any device that has support for Java—well, almost every device supports Java today.

It doesn't produce code for each type of machine, chip, and software combination out there.

That is just impossible. And even if you tried it would make Java way too large a system since you have to accommodate every type of hardware, software, and operating system there is.

So, how does the JVM do it? I

t produces its own unique code format called bytecode.

Take note that unlike other programming languages, when your Java source code is compiled it isn't directly translated or converted into machine readable language—well, again because the goal is not to make a specific type of code that can run on only one computer platform.

The Java bytecode produced by a compiler is a set of instructions that are in machine language.

Bytecode will run on any computer that has JVM installed in it. This also means that JVM runs not just Java code and Java programs, it can also run programs written in other programming languages as well—all that is needed is for those programs to be translated (aka compiled) into bytecode.

On top of that, bytecode doesn't need to be customized so that it can be understood by different devices—as long as a device has JVM then it can run bytecode. And that is how Java can run on any device and on any computer.

Now that you have learned about the important geeky stuff, we can now move on to actual coding in Java.

Writing Your First Java Code

Before you can write and run any Java program on your computer you need to install it on your computer first.

To install the Java Runtime Environment or JRE (i.e. the entire Java system with the JVM, the Java libraries, and all the other files), you need to go to the official Oracle corporate website by clicking here.

Instructions on how to download JRE will be provided in those web pages as well.

Some of the instructions will include temporarily disabling your firewall and what to expect during the installation process.

Now, your computer might prompt you that you don't have Java (the system that runs Java programs) installed on your computer, then you can download and install it by clicking here. Note: JRE is what you need to write Java programs, but your computer will need to install the actual Java system so that it can run Java programs.

Note that the link provided above is for the installer for Windows operating systems.

If you need to install Java for other operating systems like Mac OS X, Linux, and others, you should go here instead.

If for some reason those links don't work or you are taken to a different page, then just Google "JRE download" and then click on the link that has www.oracle.com on it.

Required Tools

For now all you need is a text editor to write your very first Java program code.

You can use any text editor that comes with your system (e.g. Notepad if you're using Windows).

You can also use Notepad++ if you want something that has more programming support.

IDE

However, if you want to develop applications, test your programming code, and have tools that will make programming in Java a lot easier, then you will need a program called an IDE, which stands for integrated development environment.

And IDE is an app that comes with pretty much all the facilities and tools that a programmer needs.

IDE Features

An IDE usually comes with features like autocomplete and text highlighting.

It can also be used in the building of executable files. Your Java code is usually saved as a .java file.

A compiler will then process that file and return a .class file, which is a file that you can run to test how your Java code works.

DEBUGGING

Debugging is another important feature of IDEs.

Debugging refers to location and removal of programming errors on your Java source code.

No one expects you to be perfect but programming errors will prevent your code from running. IDEs have debugging tools to help you spot the errors quickly so that you can edit them ASAP.

Best IDEs for Java Programming

There are numerous IDEs that you can use for Java programming. We can't hope to name them all so we'll just go over the top 3 IDEs.

1. NetBeans

NetBeans was first released back in 1997 and it can run on different operating systems like Windows, Solaris, Mac OS, and Linux. NetBeans is actually the official IDE for Java 8.

Just like Java, NetBeans is open source – that means it is free to download and use.

It features semantic and syntactic highlighting. It also allows you to refactor your source code (i.e. rewriting code making it more efficient without actually causing any programming problems).

Refactoring is done either to improve the performance of a program or to update it to the latest standards. In other words you are giving an old program an upgrade or update.

2. IntelliJ IDEA

IntelliJ IDEA was first released back in January of 2001. It runs on Windows, Mac OS, and Linux. This IDE comes in 2 different editions.

The first one is the proprietary aka the commercial version (i.e. the one you have to pay for) and the other one is the Apache 2 Licensed edition.

This is the IDE for really serious programmers—we suggest that you use this integrated development environment after you have gained a lot of experience programming in Java. You can call this the deep dive IDE.

Two of the unique and powerful features of IntelliJ IDEA include flow analysis and cross language refactoring. It also provides support for other JVM based languages—yes there are other programming languages that also use JVM.

3. Eclipse

Eclipse is another advanced integrated development environment.

In fact, this one is solely dedicated and specialized for the development of Java programs.

Well, it also supports other programming languages as well, which makes it a very powerful tool.

In case you have reached the point of being able to combine different programs written in different programming languages then you might want to consider getting this IDE.

If you are a beginner then that will be some time in the future. Now, there are two versions of Eclipse.

There is a cloud version of this IDE which is called Eclipse Che and there is the good old desktop version, which you can download on your computer.

Both of these versions come with an entire suite of tools, apps, and plugins that make programming work a whole lot easier. It even comes with its own custom compiler.

This IDE is loaded with a lot of useful features.

For instance, if you want to focus on developing plugins for programs that have already been written, Eclipse has a Plugin Development Environment.

It has all the tools you need to create and improve plugins.

There are a lot of other IDEs of course. You can find them by just Googling "best Java IDEs".

There are free IDEs and there are commercial ones as well. You can try the three mentioned here or you can investigate other IDEs out there.

The choice is yours.

Here's a short list of IDEs that you can find out there:
- **JDeveloper**
- **Greenfoot**
- **DrJava**
- **Codenavy**
- **Xcode**
- **MyEclipse**
- **BlueJ**

Chapter 5: Basic structure of a Java Program

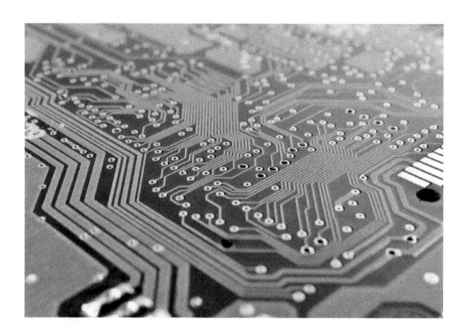

Package

On the first line, we have the statement

package helloworld;

This statement tells the compiler that the Java file we wrote belongs to the helloworld package.

A package is simply a grouping of related classes and interfaces.

When we write package helloworld; at the top of our file, we are asking the compiler to include this file in the helloworld package.

The compiler will then create a folder named "helloworld" and save the file into that folder.

Files that belong to the same package are stored in the same folder.

If you navigate to your "NetBeansProjects" folder now, you'll find a folder named "HelloWorld".

The "NetBeansProject" folder is normally located in your "Documents" folder. If you can't find this folder, try searching for it using your computer's search function.

Within the "HelloWorld" folder, you'll find a "src" folder that contains the "helloworld" folder.

In addition to packages created by us, Java also comes with a large number of pre-created packages that contain code that we can use in our programs.

For instance, code for input and output is bundled in the java.io package while code for implementing the components of a graphical user interface (like buttons, menus, etc) is bundled in the java.awt package. To use these pre-written packages, we need to import them into our programs.

We'll learn how to do that at a later time.

Within the HelloWorld class, we have the main() method which starts on line 5 and ends on line 8.

The main() Method

The main() method is the entry point of all Java applications. Whenever a Java application is started, the main() method is the first method to be called.

Notice the words String[] args inside the parenthesis of our main() method? This means the main() method can take in an array of strings as input.

In our example, the main() method contains two lines of code. The first line

//Print the words Hello World on the screen is known as a comment and is ignored by the compiler.

Chapter 6: Code structure of Java

In the figure, you should notice the package name comes first.

Additionally, you should note that a semicolon is what ends the line.

The semicolon is important and if you omit it, the program will not compile.

package firstproject;

Next is the class name

public class FirstProject {

}

You can use the left curly bracket at the start of a code, and use the right curly bracket to end the code {this is an example of a curly code segment} you should however note that anything that goes inside the left and right curly is part of the said code segment.

Additionally, anything inside both the left and right curly for the class is in fact, a code segment. Here is what I mean:

$$\text{public static void } \textbf{\textit{main}} \Big(\textbf{ String[ ] args} \Big) \Big\{$$

}

 More important than anything else is the word "main". Why?

Because each time any Java program boots up, it first looks for the method bearing the name 'main'. Simply put, a method is a piece of code.

The program then executes codes within the curly as part of the main.

There are possibilities that you will get an error message within the Java program if your code does not have a main method.

However, since this is the main entry point for your program, there is little chance you will omit it.

The public part of the code (the blue part) simply means that the method is viewable outside that class.

On the other hand, static means that the creation of a new object is not necessary while void means that, there is not returnable value and the command gets on with it.

How to download and install Java on Linux, Windows and Mac.

Check out the figure below.

Figure 10

In the NetBeans tool bar, you will notice a "green play" arrow; you can use this to run a program.

Figure 11

You can also run a program by navigating to your projects window.

This is especially effective in ensuring that the correct source code is running.

To do this, you need to click on your java source file contained in the project window and then right click for options.

Execute the run command. See figure below.

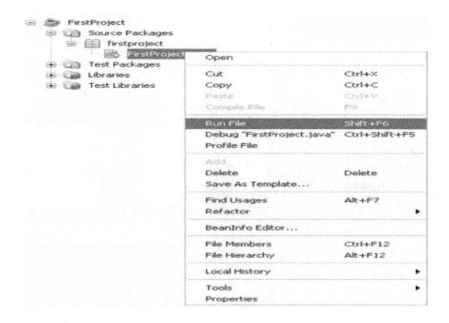

Figure 12

If you use any of the program execution methods above on our code so far, you should get something similar to figure13 below on the output window

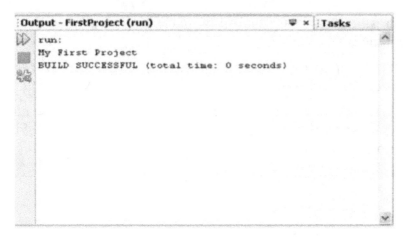

Figure 13

In figure 13 above, you can see that the first line is the run command.

The second is our code "My First Project."

If there is something you are not sure of and would like to run the code again, you can simply press the "two almost fast-forward green arrows" visible on figure 13 above.

Chapter 7: Data Types and Variables

Of course, one of the key reasons to use Java is its focus on Object – oriented programming. Object – oriented programming, or "OOP" is a type of programming language model which allows the program's code to be organized around data, rather than functions and logic, which is known as procedural programming.

These "data clusters" are organized into things called "objects", hence the moniker of "object – oriented programming".

These objects are created by something called "classes", understood here in the traditional sense of how classes are types of objects, allowing the programmer to "classify" them according to two major criteria: attributes and methods.

The attributes of a class are the raw data that will create the object: these are its descriptors, such as the values that it possesses, and other relevant data that will make up the object.

The second criterion is the "method" of the object.

This "method" is the behavior, or the logical sequences contained within the class, describing how it interacts or can be interacted with natively.

In order to make this clearer, say that there is a class "Human". This "class" will have attributes such as height, weight, gender, race. The "human" class can also have methods such as "run", "walk", "talk". These theoretical components make up the "human" class, a blueprint for an object.

Now that the class has been defined, the programmer, if they so wish, can create an object using the "human" class as a blueprint.

They can invoke the class "Human" and "populate" its attributes, giving it a specific height, weight, gender, and race. In addition, the object already has built – in functions such as "run", "walk", and "talk", so upon the creation of an object, let's say named "Mike" from the "Human" class, it already contains the functions to run, walk, and talk, without need for the programmer to code those specific functions again, as they are already "inherent" in the created object.

In a nutshell, that is what Object - oriented programming is meant to be: a way of programming that allows the programmer to draw on pre – defined classes so that it will be easier to describe them and use their internal, or built – in functions in order to operate them.

Assuming that the reader is not a total newbie to programming, and has been introduced to the world of programming using C or another procedural – heavy language, the next logical question would be: why even use object – oriented programming?

Well, one of its main advantages is that in the long run, it saves time.

Procedural programming is usually much quicker and more straightforward in simpler algorithms and programs; rather than having to construct and define a class, and create an object based on that class, all the programmer really has to do is to simply declare the necessary variables and write the functions, and create the algorithm in order to solve the problem that they need the code to address.

However, when it comes to more complex programs, needing more complex solutions, this is where object – oriented programming begins to shine, and this is where it starts to show its strength.

 In a lot of programs, there will be times that there will be a number of "objects" or data clusters that have to be grouped together, and that the programmer will be treating in a certain way.

This is what "classes" are meant to address.

Instead of declaring a new set of variables per data cluster, they can simply draw on a pre – made "class" and create a new "object".

Let's see how this would work in practice.

If a programmer were to code a chess game in procedural fashion, then they would have to manually describe each and every piece, all sixteen pawns, four bishops and four knights, four rooks, two queens, and two kings. In addition, they will have to write the functions that allow each piece to move in its own separate way.

However, if the programmer makes use of object - oriented programming, instead of having to code sixteen pawns, four bishops, four knights, four rooks, two queens, two kings, they simply have to code six classes: one class to describe each piece on the board.

The programmer can now simply include the movement functions within each class, and have the attributes describe their position: whether they're white king's pawn, or black queen's pawn, these are all things that can be inserted through the "attributes" portion of the "pawn" class. Instead of thirty – two clusters of code, the programmer only has to do six.

Now it's much easier, much shorter, and also much more elegant.

Java tokens

Java tokens are the values that are smaller than other integers.

These numbers are going to fall between the value of -32768 and 32767.

The code that I have been using is not going to work for shorts, instead I am going to need to use the short function so that I can make sure that the values are going to fall between the set limitations.

Large values are going to be stored inside of a double value along with floating point values.

A double does not have to be used if I can use a floating point. As I am storing a floating variable.

I am going to need to put a letter at the end of my value amount.

This value should be f because it is a floating point number.

Keywords

In Java, the Boolean type refers to false or true values. J

ava finds out if it is true or false using the reserved keywords. Therefore, an expression Boolean type will assume one of these values.

An example to demonstrate include:

There are a few things to note about this program.

First, the **println()**, displays a boolean value. Secondly, the boolean values control the flow of an if statement.

You don't need to go the long way in writing the boolean type this way: **if (b == true)**

The result shown by the operator such as < is boolean. It is one of the reasons why we have the expression **11 > 8** showing the value **true**.

In addition, the other pair of parentheses near the **11 > 8** is important since plus comes before the >.

Identifiers

The top layer of the diagram above is for the identifier or name.

This top layer is the name you give to a class. The name should specifically identify and also describe the type of object as seen or experienced by the user.

In simple terms, the name or identifier should identify the class.

Operators

Java has an extensive list of operator environment.

If you are wondering what an operator is, you can look at it as a symbol which conveys a specific message to the compiler to carry out a logical or mathematical operation. In Java, you will interact with four classes of operators.

The four classes include:

- Logical operator

- Bitwise operator

- Relational operator

- Arithmetic operator

Like other computer languages, Java has a defined list of additional operators to take care of certain specific scenarios.

When it comes to learning JAVA programming language, or any programming language for that matter, there are five basic concepts you must understand before you get started.

These five basic concepts include:

1. Variables
2. Data Structures
3. Control Structures
4. Syntax
5. Tools

Each of these concepts will be thoroughly explained on a beginner's level to ensure that they are understood.

Separators

They are not suitable for high-level abstraction: note that a lot of these programs make use of low-level constructs which are primarily used for low-level abstraction.

The usual approach with these programming languages is that they focus on the machine – how to make a computer do something rather than how these functions can help solve the issues of a user.

These languages deal with the minute details, which is already beyond the scope of high-level abstraction, which is the more common approach that we see today.

In low-level abstraction, data structures and algorithms are taken separately whereas these are taken as a whole in high-level abstraction.

Literals

When it comes to literals in Java, we mean the fixed values which appear in the form in which human beings can read. We can say the number 200 is a literal. Most of the time, literals can be constants.

Literals are important in a program. In fact, most Java programs use literals. Some of the programs we have already discussed in this book use literals.

Literals in Java can fall on various primitive data types.

The manner in which every literal is shown is determined by its type. Like it was mentioned some time back, we enclose character constants in single quotes such as '**c**' and '**%**'.

We define literals in integers without involving the fractional part. For instance, 12 and -30 are integer literals. A floating point literal should contain the decimal point plus the fractional part. 12.389 is a floating literal.

Java further permits for one to apply the scientific notation for the floating point literals.

Integer literals contain int value and anyone can initialize them with a variable of **short, byte,** and **char**.

comments

When this occurs, we call the grey's comments. In the running stages of the program, the grey's (comments) are moot.

This is to mean that you can use the comment feature to state or explain what the code you are creating wants to achieve.

 You can achieve this by typing two slashes and then the comment. Here is a sample.

//Place your single line comment here

You can have more than one comment line by doing either of the following:

//We are going to

//spread the comments into two

Or

/*
This comment spreads over two lines

*/

If you look at the comment above, you will notice that it starts with /* but ends with */

Additionally, if you look at the previous image (figure 8) you will notice that there are comments that begin with a single forward slash and two asterisks (/**) but end with one asterisks and one forwards slash; this is called a Javadoc comment.

what are variables

A variable, on the other hand, is an "object" that contains a specific data type and its assigned or received value.

It is called a variable because the value contained can change according to how it is used in the code, how the coder can declare its value, or even how the user of the program chooses to interact with it.

A variable, in short, is a storage unit for a data type. Having access to variables allow programmers to conveniently label and call stored values at hand.

Types of variables in Java

Java requires the programmer to use declaration statements, lines of code used to declare variables and define them by specifying the particular data type and name.

Java has a specific way of treating variables, by defining variables as containers that contains a certain type and value of information, unlike some languages such as python, which only requires a declaration of a variable, and the variable can dynamically change its type;

Java variables are **static**, which retain their type once declared.

Int number = 20;

Boolean completed = true;

String hello = "Hello World!";

The syntax in declaring is seen in the previous examples, with the type of the variable coming first, then the name of the variable, then the value.

Note as well that the declaration statement can be composed of multiple declarations in one line, as in the following example:

Int number = 20, Boolean completed = true, string hello = "Hello World!";

Java variables can be declared without any value at the start; in cases such as these, Java chooses to declare these variables with a particular default value, for example:

Byte a;

Short num;

Boolean answer;

Will result in the values 0, 0, and false, respectively.

A more complete list of default values is as follows: the byte, short, int, and long data types will all result in a default value of 0, while the float and double data types will have a default 0.0 value, the char data type will result in 'u\0000' value, a string or any other object will have a null default value, and all Booleans will begin with a false default value.

In Java, variables are static when declared, meaning that the programmer must define the data type that the variable will be containing.

To illustrate, if we wish to use a variable **num** to store a number, we would first have to declare the variable: "int **num**", before we can assign a value, such as "**num = 10".**

The process above is usually known as and referred to as an "assignment statement", where a value is **assigned** to the variable as declared by the programmer.

However, one prominent thing about how Java, and in fact how most programming languages, works is that in the assignment statement, such as in our example of num = 10, the actual value stored is the one on the right side of the equals sign, the value of 10, and num is just the "marker" to call that stored value.

This is why there are many Java programmers that tend to prefer the jargon of "getting" a value rather than "assigning", though for the most part, they may be employed interchangeably, and outside of some rare scenario, function mostly the same way.

Note, however, that once values have been assigned to variables, functions need to be carried out in order for the data inside that variable to change its data type.

Naming a variable

Creating variables is an easy task, especially given how Java programmers tend to create and name them after the data type or the purpose of what the variable will store.

However, there are a few rules when it comes to naming these variables, else Java will not recognize it and an error message will result. The main restrictions around variable names are that it should not begin with a special character such as an underscore or a number.

However, variable names can consist of characters such as letters and numbers, and even an underscore, provided that the underscore is not placed at the start.

No other characters may be used, such as the # or even $, as these special characters have different uses in Java, and thus will not be recognized in a variable name.

While those are the major rules, here are some tips when it comes to naming variables.

The variable name should be descriptive, as in longer codes it may be difficult to recall just what "x" is for.

Having a variable name such as "count" or "output" is much easier to recall as compared to having a generic "x" or "y" and will help in avoiding confusion.

In addition to being descriptive, variables will also be easier to use if their names are kept fairly short.

While having a variable name such as banking_information_account_records is very descriptive, typing it repeatedly as needed in the program will get exhausting, and having longer variable names increase the chances of typographical errors, which will lead to bugs in the code, resulting in a run - time error or the code not working as intended, or working, but introducing bugs along the way.

Note as well that it has always been a practice for Java variables to be written in all lower – case letters, and while there is no restriction on capitalization, keeping things in lowercase simplifies things, as a missed capitalization may result in the variable not being recognized, as Java reads an upper – case letter as an entirely different character versus a lower – case letter.

Java primitive types

Method Naming Conventions

We shall revisit the naming conventions in Java since you will be using member methods.

Methods in Java programming perform operations, they also receive any argument provided by a caller, and it can also return a result of an operation to a caller.

Here's the syntax for declaring a method:

[Access Control Modifier] Return Type methodName ([set of parameters]) {

   // body of the method

   ......

}

Here are a few rules to remember when you make the names for the methods that you will write.

Method names are always verbs or more specifically verb phrases (which means you can use multiple words to name them).

The first word of the method name should all be in lower case letters while the rest of the words should follow a camel case format. Here is an example:

writeMethodNamesThisWay( )

Now, you should remember that verbs are used for method names, and they indicate an action while nouns are used for variable names, and they denote a certain attribute.

Following the syntax for declaring a method and following the name conventions for this Java construct, here's a sample code that can be used to compute the area of a circle.

```
public double computeCircleArea() {
return radius * radius * Math.PI;
}
```

Using Constructors in Your Code

We'll just go over some additional details as they relate to object oriented programming.

As stated earlier, a constructor will look like a method, and you can certainly think of it and treat it like a special kind of method in Java programming.

However, a constructor will still be different from a method in several ways. The name of a constructor will be the same as the class name.

Use the keyword or operator "new" to create a new instance of the constructor and also to initialize it. Here's an example using the class "Employee" and a variety of ways to initialize it in your code:

```
Employee payrate1 = new Employee( );
Employee payrate2 = new Employee(2.0);
Employee payrate3 = new Employee(3.0, "regular");
```

A constructor will also implicitly return void – that simply means it doesn't have a return type. You can't put a return statement inside the body of a constructor since it will be flagged by compilers as an error.

The only way you can invoke a constructor is via the use of the "new" statement. We have already given you several ways how you can invoke constructors in the samples above.

One final difference is that constructors can't be inherited. Let's go back to the examples provided above – the first line includes "Employee( );" – that is called a default constructor. As you can see, it has no parameters whatsoever.

The job of a default constructor is to simply initialize the member variables to a specific default value. In the example above, the member variable payrate1 was initialized to its default pay rate and employee status.

Can constructors be overloaded too? Yes, they can. Constructors behave like methods too so that means you can overload a constructor just the same way you overload a method.

Here are a few examples on how you can overload a constructor.

We use the Employee class and overload it using different parameters.

Employee( )

Employee(int r)

Employee(int r, String b)

How to initialize a variable

Now that we know how to declare variables, and we know the various types of variables that are available to us, the next thing to do is to learn how to make use of these variables, in something called "expressions".

Expressions are the most used building blocks of a Java program, generally meant to produce a new value as a result, though in some cases expressions are used to assign a new value to a variable.

Generally, expressions are made up of things such as values, variables, operators, and method calls.

There are also some expressions that produce no result, but rather affect another variable.

One example would be an expression that changes the value of a variable based on an operation: there is no new value output, and there is no true "assignment" of a new value, but rather there is what is called a **side effect** that results in a changed variable value.

In our previous sample program above, such as the "Hello World" printing program, we introduced raw values into the print function, also known as "hard coding" the output.

However, at this point, we should try to incorporate what we have learned about variables.

Variables operate much the same way as raw values, as they simply reference a previously stored value by the computer, and as such, the programmer can just use the variable name instead of the value.

In order to demonstrate this, let us remember the previous "Hello World" program:

print ("Hello World") ;

input ("\n\nPlease press the return key to close this window.") ;

Now, instead of hard – coding the "Hello World" string, we can simply declare it into a variable and have the program output that variable.

This should end up looking as:

String = "Hello World" ;

print(string) ;

input ("\n\nPlease press the return key to close this window.") ;

This should come out with the same result as the previous program, looking something similar to:

Hello World

Please press the return key to close this window.

Variables modified by code

However, the reader may be wondering why we even use a variable in this case, as it makes our code even longer.

In very short codes, such as the classic "Hello World", using variables does make it longer, but to demonstrate how they can be used to shorten a code, let's use another code to show the usefulness of variables.

For this code, we will attempt to print out a few times table values. In this code we will be using a few iterations and loops, which will be explained further on.

Int num = 9;

byte count = 0 ;

while (counter <10) {

print(num " * ") ;

print(counter "= ") ;

```
print(num * counter "\n") ;

counter = counter + 1} ;
```

This basic snippet of code will output the multiplication table of whatever is in the num variable up until times nine. In this program we are to be incorporating a so – called while condition and an iteration function.

However, if we break down the components of the code as provided, the "while" condition tells Java to continue iterating the code beneath it until the condition is not true. Since count was initialized at a value of 0, and every time the code runs, the count variable will increase by one, the loop will run for ten times.

The code nested within the "while" condition tells the Java program to print an equation of the number multiplied by the "counter" variable, meaning that it will print ten lines, from times zero to times nine.

The code should end up looking like the following output:

$9 * 0 = 0$

$9 * 1 = 9$

$9 * 2 = 18$

$9 * 3 = 27$

$9 * 4 = 36$

$9 * 5 = 45$

$9 * 6 = 54$

$9 * 7 = 63$

$9 * 8 = 72$

$9 * 9 = 81$

Now try and imagine how a more seasoned programmer would think of how to write an algorithm to create a similar table without having a variable that can be changed as the code runs.

They would have to "hard – code" all the values and type all the numbers just to get a simple multiplication table. However, due to the power of variables, the coder can simply assign a basic starting value and their code should do the rest.

Variables modified by user input

Variables can have a value declared by the programmer in the code, but the programmer can also have their variables as defined by the user.

Remember that user input can be read by the Python code by the use of the input () function.

They can do this while declaring the variable, or they may wish to have their user input a new value to an already – declared variable.

Let's see how this works using the previous multiplication table code:

```
Int num = NextInt(input("Please enter a number from 0 – 9 to initialize the multiplication table.")) ;
Int counter = 0 ;
while (counter<10){
print(num " * ") ;
print(counter "= ") ;
print(num * counter "\n") ;
counter = counter + 1 ; }
```

This code prints an initial line and waits for the user to input a number before the code will run.

Note that the user can technically enter a character that is not a number, and this will result in an error.

Furthermore, the input function in this case is limited to receiving a single character, so only a number from 0 – 9 can be used, as longer digits will not be read.

The variable declaration is a nested function, ensuring that the user input will be converted into an integer, rather than having a character, allowing the code to use mathematical operations.

Arithmetic operators

Arithmetic operators in Java include:

- + represents addition
- - represents subtraction
- * represents multiplication
- / represents division
- % represents modulus
- ++ represents increment
- -- represents decrement

Operators such as +, -, *, and / all perform the same function just like the rest of other languages.

> We have seen that JavaScript has the ability to work with numbers. Hence it also has the ability to work with the operators that can be used with the number data type. Let's look at each of the operators in more detail.

Arithmetic Operators

These are operators that are used to work with numbers. The most common operators are shown below, followed by an example of how it can be applied.

With this program, the output is as follows:

JavaScript Program

The first value is 5

The second value is 10

Addition operator = 15

Subtraction operator = 5

Multiply operator = 50

Division operator = 2

Increment operator = 6

Decrement operator = 5

Modulus operator = 5

Assignment operators

These are operators that are used to determine the value of conditions based on the value of the operands.

The relational operators possible in JavaScript are given below.

If a condition evaluates to true, then a value of 1 is returned, otherwise a value of 0 is returned.

With this program, the output is as follows:

JavaScript Program

The first value is 5

The second value is 10

Are the numbers equal = false

Are the numbers not equal = true

Is x less than y = true

Is x greater than y = false

Is x greater than or equal y = false

Is x less than or equal y = true

Logical Operators

These are operators that are used to determine the value of conditions based on the value of the operands, where the operands are Boolean values.

The logical operators possible in JavaScript are given below.

With this program, the output is as follows:

JavaScript Program

The first value is true

The second value is true

The third value is false

x AND y = true

y AND z = false

z AND x = false

z AND z = false

The table below shows the logical operators based on the value of the operands for the OR operator.

With this program, the output is as follows:

JavaScript Program

The first value is true

The second value is true

The third value is false

x OR y = true

y OR z = true

z OR x = true

z OR z = false

The following table shows the logical operators based on the value of the operands for the NOT operator.

Assignment Operators

These are operators that are used to make assignment operations easier. The assignment operators possible in JavaScript are given below.

Now let's look at how we can implement these operators in further detail.

With this program, the output is as follows:

JavaScript Program

The first value is 5

The second value is 6

The value of i+j is 11

The value of i+=j is 11

The value of i-=j is 5

The value of i*=j is 30

The value of i/=j is 5

The value of i%=j is 5

Bitwise Operators

These are operators that are used to make bit operations on operands.

With this program, the output is as follows:

JavaScript Program

The first value is 5

The second value is 6

The value of x AND y is 4

The value of x OR y is 7

The value of NOT x is -6

The value of x XOR y is 3

The value Zero fill left shift is 10

The value Signed right shift is 2

The value Zero fill right shift is 2

Chapter 8: Java Data Structure and Algorithms

In order to make this clearer, say that there is a class "Human". This "class" will have attributes such as height, weight, gender, race. The "human" class can also have methods such as "run", "walk", "talk".

These theoretical components make up the "human" class, a blueprint for an object. Now that the class has been defined, the programmer, if they so wish, can create an object using the "human" class as a blueprint.

They can invoke the class "Human" and "populate" its attributes, giving it a specific height, weight, gender, and race.

In addition, the object already has built – in functions such as "run", "walk", and "talk", so upon the creation of an object, let's say named "Mike" from the "Human" class, it already contains the functions to run, walk, and talk, without need for the programmer to code those specific functions again, as they are already "inherent" in the created object.

In a nutshell, that is what Object - oriented programming is meant to be: a way of programming that allows the programmer to draw on pre – defined classes so that it will be easier to describe them and use their internal, or built – in functions in order to operate them.

Assuming that the reader is not a total newbie to programming, and has been introduced to the world of programming using C or another procedural – heavy language, the next logical question would be: why even use object – oriented programming?

Well, one of its main advantages is that in the long run, it saves time.

Procedural programming is usually much quicker and more straightforward in simpler algorithms and programs; rather than having to construct and define a class, and create an object based on that class, all the programmer really has to do is to simply declare the necessary variables and write the functions, and create the algorithm in order to solve the problem that they need the code to address.

However, when it comes to more complex programs, needing more complex solutions, this is where object – oriented programming begins to shine, and this is where it starts to show its strength.

In a lot of programs, there will be times that there will be a number of "objects" or data clusters that have to be grouped together, and that the programmer will be treating in a certain way.

This is what "classes" are meant to address. Instead of declaring a new set of variables per data cluster, they can simply draw on a pre – made "class" and create a new "object". Let's see how this would work in practice.

If a programmer were to code a chess game in procedural fashion, then they would have to manually describe each and every piece, all sixteen pawns, four bishops and four knights, four rooks, two queens, and two kings.

In addition, they will have to write the functions that allow each piece to move in its own separate way.

However, if the programmer makes use of object - oriented programming, instead of having to code sixteen pawns, four bishops, four knights, four rooks, two queens, two kings, they simply have to code six classes: one class to describe each piece on the board.

The programmer can now simply include the movement functions within each class, and have the attributes describe their position: whether they're white king's pawn, or black queen's pawn, these are all things that can be inserted through the "attributes" portion of the "pawn" class. Instead of thirty – two clusters of code, the programmer only has to do six.

Now it's much easier, much shorter, and also much more elegant.

Chapter 9: Arrays in Java

Arrays are sequences of elements; each element must be associated with one or more index positions.

Elements are groups of memory locations, each one storing one item of data.

Indexes are integers that are non-negative; in the case of the array, they are used for identifying the element associated with the index.

You can consider the relationship between the two to be similar to how a postbox number identifies a specific house on a specific street.

Usually, one element will have one index but there may sometimes be more.

The number of those indexes per element is the dimension of the array.

We are going to start by looking at one-dimensional arrays; later, we will move on to the multi-dimensional arrays.

Java has full support for arrays. Each of the elements in an array will occupy the same byte amount and the exact amount will depend on the data type of the element.

It is also worth noting at this stage that every element in one array will be of the same data type.

It is also important to note that you cannot resize a Java array; they are of a fixed size and may not be changed once they have been created.

Rather than doing this, if you needed an array to be a different size, you would need to create a new one of the correct size and then copy all the elements you need from the first array to the new one.

One-Dimensional Arrays

One-dimensional arrays are the simplest of all arrays.

In this kind of array, one element is associated with one index and the array is used for storing data items in lists.

We can use three separate techniques for creating a one-dimensional array:

- With just an initializer
- With just the new keyword
- With both an initializer and the new keyword

Using Just an Initializer

The syntax required to use an initializer to create a one-dimensional array is:

'{' [expr (',' expr)*] '}'

What this syntax says is that a one-dimensional array is a list of expressions that is optional and with each expression separated by a comma, all between a set of curly braces.

All of the expressions have got to evaluate to types that are compatible.

For example, if you had a one-dimensional array of doubles with two elements, both of those elements may be of the double type or just one may be of the double type while the other may be an integer or a floating point number.

Have a look at this example:

{ 'J', 'a', 'v', 'a' }

Using the New Keyword

The new keyword is used to allocate the array memory and return the array references. The syntax is:

'new' type '[' int_expr ']'

What the syntax tells us is that the one-dimensional array is a series of positive elements, all of int (integer) type.

All the elements in the array will be zeroed and will be interpreted as one of the following:

- 0
- 0L
- 0.0F
- 0.0
- false
- null
- '\u0000'

For example:

new char[4]

Using an Initializer and the New Keyword

The syntax required to create the array using both the initializer and the new keyword is this, a combination of the two separate syntax approaches mentioned above:

'new' type '[' ']' '{' [expr (',' expr)*] '}'

Because we can work out how many elements are in the one-dimensional array by looking at the list of comma-separated expressions, we do not need and, indeed, must nor use, an int_expr within the set of square brackets.

For example:

new char[] { 'J', 'a', 'v', 'a' }

It is worth noting that there is no difference between the syntax for using just the initializer and the syntax for using the initializer and the new keyword.

The first one, with just the initializer, is something called syntactic sugar – this just means the syntax is much easier to use.

Array Variables

On its own, a new one-dimensional array is quite useless. For it to be worth anything, we must first assign its reference to an array variable that has a compatible type and we can do this in two ways – directly or by using a method call.

The following example shows how the variable is declared:

type var_name '[' ']'

type '[' ']' var_name

Both types of syntax are declaring the variable that will store the reference to the one-dimensional array. You can use whichever type you prefer but the preferred method is the first one, with the set of square brackets after the variable type.

In these examples, there are three array variables – name1, name2, and name3. The set of square brackets is telling Java that each of those variables will store the reference to a one-dimensional array.

The keyword, char, is an indication that the elements must store values of the char type but, provided Java can do a conversion to a char, you may specify values that are non-char. For example, the following is perfectly ok because 10, a positive int, is small enough that it fits in the range for char (o to 65535) and can easily be converted to a char:

char[] chars = { 'A', 10 };

However, the next example would not be ok because it doesn't fit in the range:

char[] chars = { 'A', 80000 };

All array variables have a length property associated with them. This property will return the one-dimensional array length, indicated as a positive int.

For example, name1.lenght would return a value of 4.

With the array variable specified, it is possible to access any one of the elements in the array and we do this by stating the expression that will agree with this syntax:

array_var '[' index ']'

In this expression, we have a positive int of index; it ranges from 0 to one lower than the length property value. Don't forget, Java indexes start at zero.

Have a look at a couple of examples:

char ch = names[0]; // Get value.

names[1] = 'A';   // Set value.

If a negative index is specified, or one that is >= (greater than or equal to) the value that the length property returns, Java will create an exception object and throw it. That exception object is:

java.lang.ArrayIndexOutOfBoundsException

Chapter 10: Strings in Java

A string is nothing more than a sequence of characters that is terminated by the null character, to denote that the string has indeed been terminated.

In Java a string is denoted by the string data type.

Let's revisit how to define a string in Java via an example.

With the above program:

We are first defining a variable 'str' to be of the 'string' type.

Then we assign a string of "Hello World" to the 'str' variable.

Finally we output the value to the console accordingly.

With this program, the output is as follows:

The value of the string is Hello World

There are a variety of functions available in Java to work with strings. Let's look at them in more detail.

4.1 Length Function

This function is used to return the length of the string. Let's look at an example of this function.

With the above program:

We are using the 'length' method to get the length of the string.

With this program, the output is as follows:

The length of the string is 11

4.2 toLowerCase Function

This function returns the string in lower case. Let's now look at a simple example of this.

With this program, the output is as follows:

The lower case of the string is hello world

4.3 toUpperCase Function

This function returns the string in upper case. Let's quickly look at an example of this.

With this program, the output is as follows:

The lower case of the string is HELLO WORLD

4.4 Contains Function

This function is used to check the existence of another string, and returns True or False. Below is an example of this function.

With this program, the output is as follows:

Does the string contain Hello - True

4.5 endsWith Function

This function can be used to check whether a string ends with a particular string value. Let's now look at a simple example of this function.

With this program, the output is as follows:

Does the string end with World - true

4.6 indexOf Function

This function is used to get the index of a character in a string. Let's have a look at an example of this.

With this program, the output is as follows:

The index value of e is 1

4.7 Replace Function

This function is used to replace a character in the original string. Below we'll look at an example of this function.

With this program, the output is as follows:

The value of the string is Hello Again

4.8 Substring Function

This function is used to return a substring from the original string. Let's look at a quick example of this function.

With this program, the output is as follows:

The value of the string is Hello

If the value is less than zero it means that the destination string precedes the value.

If the value is greater than zero it means that the destination string follows the value.

If the value is equal to zero then this instance has the same position in the sort order as the value.

Let's now look at an example of this function.

With this program, the output is as follows:

The output of the compareTo function is 0

Chapter 11: Java Web Development

What are Java Web Applications?

Java web applications are, quite simply, web apps built using Java. But, much more than that, they are applications that generate web pages that are fully interactive, each containing different markup language types, such XML, HTML, and so on, along with dynamic content.

Typically, a Java web application will be made up of web components that modify data temporarily store the data, interact with web services and with databases and will render content as requested by the application users.

Some of the components are JSP – JavaServer Pages, JavaBeans and servlets.

Many of the tasks that are required for the development of web applications can be somewhat repetitive or they may require huge amounts of boilerplate code.

We can use web frameworks to take away some of the overhead that goes with the common development activities, for example, many of the frameworks include useful libraries that help you with page templating, session management and they often promote the reuse of code.

What is Java EE?

Java Enterprise Edition (Java EE) is one of the most commonly used platforms and it contains a range of coordinated technologies that take some of the complexity and cost out of the development of server-centric, multi-tier applications, making it much easier to deploy them and manage them.

Java EE builds on Java SE and gives us a full set of development APIs that help us run server-side applications that are fully secure, portable scalable, robust, and reliable.

Some of the basic components include:

• EJB (Enterprise JavaBeans) – fully managed server-side architecture for enclosing application business logic. With EJB technology, we can rapidly develop Java-based applications that are distributed, secure, transactional and portable in a simplified way

• JPA (Java Persistence API) – a framework that provides ORM (Object-Relational Mapping) for data management capabilities within applications built using Java technology.

Ajax Development with JavaScript

JavaScript is used mainly in the client-side user interfaces in web applications and is an object-oriented language.

Ajax, with stands for Asynchronous JavaScript and XML, is a technique that provides the ability for web pages to change without having to refresh the page each time.

JavaScript toolkits can easily be used to implement components enabled by Ajax, along with their functionality, right into a web page.

The Practicalities of Developing Web Applications

Now it's time to get practical because that's the only real way to learn how to build a web application in Java. We're going to look at the basics of using the NetBeans IDE, how to produce a very simple web application, how to deploy it and how to see it in a web browser.

This application will use a JSP page for name input and a JavaBeans component to ensure the name persists throughout the HTTP session, retrieving that name so it can be output on the next JSP page.

The first place to start is in setting up your environment so you can follow along.

The software and resources you will need are:

- The NetBeans IDE – v 7.2 onwards, Java EE
- Java Development Kit – v 7 onwards
- Glassfish Server Open Source Edition v 4 onwards OR
- Tomcat Servlet container v 7 onwards OR
- Oracle Web Logic Server – v 10 onwards

If you opt for the Java EE version, you can easily install both the Glassfish and Apache Tomcat servlet containers.

Set Up Your Project

Once you have downloaded everything from above, you can follow this tutorial. Start by opening the NetBeans IDE

Click on File>New Project in the main menu or click CTRL+SHIFT+N if you prefer to use keyboard shortcuts.

Now click on Categories and choose Java Web

Click Projects>Web Application>Next

Go to the text box for Project Name and call it HelloWeb.

Decide the Project Location – it can be any directory on your system. For this tutorial we will be referring to the directory as $PROJECTHOME.

This is an optional step – check the box beside Use the Dedicated Folder for Storing Libraries and decide where the libraries folder will go.

Click on Next and a panel for the Server and Settings will open. Choose which Java EE version you are going to use with the application

Next, choose which server you are going to use for deployment of your application.

Note that you will only see those servers that are registered with the NetBeans IDE. Also note the Context Path (on server) changes to /HelloWeb/ - this is indicative of the name you provided earlier.

Click on Finish

NetBeans IDE will now create a project folder called $PROJECTHOME/HelloWeb.

If you go to the Files window in NetBeans or press CTRL+2, you can see the file structure for this project; go to the Projects window, or press CTRL+1 and you can see the logical structure.

This project folder is where all of your metadata and source will go for this project. HelloWeb will open directly in NetBeans IDE while the Welcome page, which is index.jsp, will open in the main window in the Source Editor.

Note – The NetBeans IDE may generate the default welcome page as index.html but this will depend on which server and which version of the Java EE that you chose when the project was created. You have two choices – follow this tutorial using the index.html file or go to the New File wizard and create an index.jsp file – if you choose the latter, make sure you delete index.html to avoid confusion.

Create and Edit Application Source Files

The NetBeans IDE serves many useful functions but one of the most important is the creation and editing of the source files for your web application.

That, in all honesty, is what most web app developers spend the bulk of their time doing.

With the IDE, you get a huge selection of tools that will suit all types of developer and the individual style that they have, regardless of whether you prefer the IDE to generate much of the code or whether you prefer to code manually.

Chapter 12: Making our Program Interactive

How to displaying output

The floating type represents fractional numbers. The floating types exist in two types, the double and float. The double represents the double precision numbers while the float represents the single precision numbers.

The double is applied frequently since functions of mathematics use double value. For instance, sqrt() will output a double. You can check its application in the code below. In this example, sqrt() has been applied to calculate the longest side of a triangle when the length of the other sides has been provided.

```
/*
    Use the Pythagorean theorem to
    find the length of the hypotenuse
    given the lengths of the two opposing
    sides.
*/
class Hypot {
  public static void main(String args[]) {
    double x, y, z;

    x = 3;
    y = 4;                    Notice how sqrt() is called. It is preceded by
                              the name of the class of which it is a member.
    z = Math.sqrt(x*x + y*y);

    System.out.println("Hypotenuse is " +z);
  }
}
```

The output from the program is shown here:

```
Hypotenuse is 5.0
```

We need to notice in the example above that **sqrt()** belongs to the **Math** class. But, notice the way the **sqrt()** has been used: first, it has been preceded by the **Math** name. Now, for **sqrt()**, it is similar.

Converters

If you have programmed in another language, you might be thinking that characters in Java are 8. No! Java has Unicode. What a Unicode does is to define a set of characters which represents characters existing in the human languages.

The example below demonstrates:

Char th;

th = 'Y';

Still, if you want to display a char value by applying the **println()** statement. This example will show you how to do it:

```
System.out.println("This is th: "+ th);
Given that the char is unsigned 16-bit type, you can do some arithmetic operations
in the char variable. For instance, look at the program below:

Class CharArith {
Public static void main (String args []) {
Char th;
th = 'X';
System.out.println("th has "+ th);
th++; // we increment the th, it is possible to increment a char
System.out.println("th is now "+ th);
th = 90; // we assign th the value Z
System.out.println("th is now "+ th);
}
}
Here is the output of the above program:
"th has X"
"th is now Y"
"th is now Z"
```

This program assigns variable **th** the value '**X**'. Then, it is incremented to **Y**, which is the next character in the Unicode sequence.

Formatting outputs

In Java, the Boolean type refers to false or true values. Java finds out if it is true or false using the reserved keywords. Therefore, an expression

Boolean type will assume one of these values. An example to demonstrate include:

```
class BoolPro {
public static void main (String args []) {
 boolean q;
q = false;
System.out.println ("q is "+ q);
q= true;
System.out.println("q is "+ q);
// a boolean value can also control the if statement
If(q)
System.out.println("This is executed.");
q = false;
if(q)
System.out.println("This is not executed");
// Describe the results of the relational operator
System.out.println("11 > 8 is "+ (10 > 8));
}
}
The output:
 q is false
q is true
This is executed
11 > 8 is true
```

There are a few things to note about this program.

First, the **println(),** displays a boolean value. Secondly, the boolean values control the flow of an if statement.

You don't need to go the long way in writing the boolean type this way: **if (b == true)**

The result shown by the operator such as < is boolean. It is one of the reasons why we have the expression **11 > 8** showing the value **true**. In addition, the other pair of parentheses near the **11 > 8** is important since plus comes before the >.

Escape sequences

Surrounding them with single quotes works for the majority of printing characters. However, there are certain characters which have a problem with the text editor.

Furthermore, double and single quotes tend to have a unique meaning to Java. T

his means you cannot just use them directly. Now, because of the above reason, Java has specific escape sequences, sometimes it is called a **backslash character constant**. This table illustrates:

Escape Sequence	Description
\'	Single quote
\"	Double quote
\\	Backslash
\r	Carriage return
\n	New line
\f	Form feed
\t	Horizontal tab
\b	Backspace
\ddd	Octal constant (where ddd is an octal constant)
\uxxxx	Hexadecimal constant (where xxxx is a hexadecimal constant)

Chapter 13: Control Flow Statements

When we talk about conditional logic, we are mostly talking about the IF word.

For example, IF user is younger than 18 then display this message; IF user is older than 18, display this message. Luckily, you will find that using conditional logic in Java is easy so let's begin by looking at IF statements.

IF Statements

One of the most common things in computer programming is to execute code when one thing happens instead of something else.

Run the program and check it – Note that NetBeans tends to run the program in bold text in the window for Projects, not the code that you displayed.

If you want the code run in your coding window, right-click on the code, anywhere and then click on **Run File** in the menu that appears. The output will now appear in the Output window.

Next, we change the user variable value from 17 to 18; now run the program again.

You should see that the program runs fine, no errors but nothing will be printed.

The reason for this is because the message is in between the curly brackets in the IF statement and that statement is looking for values of lower than 18. If the condition isn't met, Java will ignore the curly brackets and anything in between them, moving on to the rest of the code.

Nested ifs

We have previously looked at nested scopes; now we want to look at nested ifs. You will interact most of the time with a nested if. The greatest lesson to learn is nested ifs point to the block of code with the else.

Read the following example:

```
If( i ==10) {
If ( j < 20) a = b;
If (k > 100) c = d;
else a - c; // this else will point to the if (k > 100)
}
else a = d; //this else will point to the if (i ==10)
```

You should be able to note that the last else has not been associated with if(j<20), but associated with the if(i==10).

IF ... ELSE

If you don't want to use two IF statements, there is another way -and IF ... ELSE statement.

So, we have two choices in this code – the user is either 18 or younger, or older than 18.

Change your code so it matches what is above and try it.

You should now see that the first message is printed out. Change the user variable value to 20 and then run the code again.

You should see the message that is between the curly brackets for ELSE displayed in the Output window.

IF ... ELSE IF

The first IF statement will test for the first condition, then we have the ELSE IF, followed by parentheses, in between which goes condition two. If there is anything that the first two conditions do not catch, it will be caught by the last ELSE. Again, we have sectioned the code using curly brackets and each IF, Else IF or ELSE has its own set. If you miss out any of these curly brackets, you will get an error message.

Before you try out any more code, you must first learn about a few more conditional operators. So far, you have used these ones:

- **< - Greater Than**
- **< - Less Than**
- **>= - Greater Than or Equal To**
- <u>**<= - Less Than or Equal To**</u>

Here's four more you can use:

- **&& - AND**
- **|| - OR**
- **== - HAS A VALUE OF**
- **! - NOT**

The first one, a pair of ampersand symbols, is used for testing two or more conditions at once.

We are checking to see if a user is older than the age of 18 but younger than the age of 40 – remember, we are checking what is in the variable called user.

The first condition, "greater than 18"; the second condition, "less than 40". Between those two conditions, we have the AND operator so the entire line is saying else if user is greater than 18 AND user is less than 40.

Now run the program and test it again; before it runs you should already be able to guess what is going to print.

The user variable has a value of 21 so the message that is between the else if curly brackets will show in the output window.

Nested IF Statements

Look at where the curly brackets are – get one set in the wrong place or miss one out and the code will not run. Nested IF statements might be a little tricky but, really, all you are doing is narrowing the choices down.

Boolean Values

Instead of using int, double or string, you would simply type in boolean (lower case b) and, after the variable name, you assign a TRUE or FALSE value.

Notice that we use a single equal sign as the assignment operator.

If you wanted to see if a variable "has a value of", you would need to use a pair of equals signs.

This time, we have used the NOT operator in front of the variable called user.

The NOT operator is indicated by the use of an exclamation mark, just one, and it will be placed in front of the variable that you are trying to test.

This operator tests for negation, which means that it is testing for the opposite of the actual value.

Switch Statements

Another way of controlling flow is to use a switch statement. This provides you with the option of testing for a range of values for the variables and can be used in place of complicated, long IF ... ELSE statements.

Start with the word "switch" and then a set of parentheses. The variable you are checking is placed between the switch parentheses and is followed by a set of curly brackets.

The rest of the switch statement goes in between the curly brackets.

Chapter 14: Java GUI Programming

Assuming that the reader is not a total newbie to programming, and has been introduced to the world of programming using C or another procedural – heavy language, the next logical question would be: why even use object – oriented programming?

Well, one of its main advantages is that in the long run, it saves time.

How to build a small game with Java

Procedural programming is usually much quicker and more straightforward in simpler algorithms and programs; rather than having to construct and define a class, and create an object based on that class, all the programmer really has to do is to simply declare the necessary variables and write the functions, and create the algorithm in order to solve the problem that they need the code to address.

However, when it comes to more complex programs, needing more complex solutions, this is where object – oriented programming begins to shine, and this is where it starts to show its strength. In a lot of programs, there will be times that there will be a number of "objects" or data clusters that have to be grouped together, and that the programmer will be treating in a certain way.

This is what "classes" are meant to address. Instead of declaring a new set of variables per data cluster, they can simply draw on a pre – made "class" and create a new "object". Let's see how this would work in practice.

Each piece also has different methods of moving, depending on what piece they are.

If a programmer were to code a chess game in procedural fashion, then they would have to manually describe each and every piece, all sixteen pawns, four bishops and four knights, four rooks, two queens, and two kings.

In addition, they will have to write the functions that allow each piece to move in its own separate way.

However, if the programmer makes use of object - oriented programming, instead of having to code sixteen pawns, four bishops, four knights, four rooks, two queens, two kings, they simply have to code six classes: one class to describe each piece on the board.

The programmer can now simply include the movement functions within each class, and have the attributes describe their position: whether they're white king's pawn, or black queen's pawn, these are all things that can be inserted through the "attributes" portion of the "pawn" class. Instead of thirty – two clusters of code, the programmer only has to do six.

Now it's much easier, much shorter, and also much more elegant.

Chapter 15: Object Oriented Programming

We're not going to tackle all the complex coding of object-oriented programming right now.

We're just going to be dealing with the raw concepts at heart: classes and objects. In order to understand these, we must first discuss classes.

This will make some of the things that we said earlier – like object wrappers – make more sense.

What is a class?

The utility of classes comes from the fact that sometimes you need more complex structures than what the code automatically gives you.

This occurs rarely in languages like JavaScript. Object-oriented programming is about this abstraction at its core:

the ability to take smaller concepts and then integrate them into bigger structures that utilize these concepts.

A better way to think about it is to try to imagine a dog.

All dogs have features in common; for example, they have 2 eyes, 4 legs, and a wagging tail.

They can also bark. However, there can be a lot of variance, too.

For example, dogs can have separate breeds and other things which set them apart, like their size or weight.

However, there are still unifying concepts and properties that apply to all dogs, regardless their breed, size, and weight, which are **properties** they all have in common.

These can be portrayed as individual data members of a larger structure. This structure can be referred to as a **dog**.

These individual data members are called the properties of the dog class.

Each class can also have standard functions, like **bark** or **wagTail**, which are common among all instances of the class.

A singular instance of a class is referred to as an object.

Each object has its own name and can be treated as its own variable. So, if you define a class **dog**, you can create a dog variable known as **myDog** or any other standard variable name.

Then, access the properties and alter them however you wish.

This standardization and abstraction are the major appeals of object-oriented programming.

Therefore, whenever something is referred to as an **object**, it means that a class was constructed which consists of smaller data types and pieces of data that all make up the bigger concept that is represented both through the object and through its constituent class.

With that, we've worked through the bulk of the stuff that you need to know as an new JavaScript programmer.

These are the foundations of all the knowledge you gained from this book, and it's important that you understand all these before continuing.

Java encapsulation

Information hiding is one of the key features of the Java programming language and object oriented programming. You have already been introduced to this concept in part we covered concepts on data abstraction. Simply put, an object in Java will usually hide how it implements its own functionality.

Now, in order to do that, you will have to make use of access control modifiers. Here are four of them:

- Public

- Private

- Protected

- Default

You are already familiar with the first two – public and private.

When the variable is declared to be public then it can be anywhere in the program you are writing. In contrast when it is private then it can't be seen or accessed anywhere else but in the body of the class where it has been instantiated.

Let's move on to the other two access control modifiers.

The next one on the list is called "protected" – which is useful in case you want to create libs. When a variable is protected, it means that it can only be seen within the package where this Java construct has been instantiated – note that this also includes all the subclasses.

The "default" access control modifier, on the other hand, is used by the variable when the other three aren't specified. In this mode, a variable can be accessed within package or class where it has been instantiated by the programmer. However, do take note that the variable is only accessible within the main body of the class and it is not available within its subclasses.

Note that you can also create an object within a method and the usual rules apply – the object or variable can only be accessed within the body of the method where it has been created.

Here's another important point that you should remember about variables that you create within a method – it can only specify one keyword for it: final.

You will not be allowed to create a default, protected, public, or even a private variable within the method body. And that is basically how information is hidden in your code, which, if you observe, facilitates data abstraction and encapsulation.

Encapsulation? Information Hiding? What's the Difference? It would appear at first glance that encapsulation and data or information hiding may look the same, but there is indeed a subtle difference between these two terms.

Now, Nat Pryce and Steve Freeman has made quite an accurate distinction between these two although you may read from other authors who use these terms interchangeably.

We'll use Freeman and Pryce's descriptions here to draw the difference between these two concepts in Java programming. Let's begin with information hiding since that is where we left off.

You can already judge what "information hiding" means. It simply means information is concealed. The actual functions and procedures performed by the program are concealed.

But, for what purpose? Why are the inner workings kept hidden from the programmer?

The lower level details are ignored so that you, the programmer, can focus on much more important things. That is also why data is abstracted in Java.

You can create classes, objects, and other elements of your program; you can even import objects from one program to another without worrying about the details on how that object does what it does.

It's like driving a car.

All you need to know is that when you insert your key into the keyhole and start the car, it will start.

You don't have to worry about what makes it start, how the wires are connected underneath there, where the gas goes, how the engine burns the gas, etc.

All you need to worry about is starting the car and driving safely.

Encapsulation, on the other hand, allows the user to control the amount of change in an object can affect the other parts of class.

The term "encapsulate" means to enclose everything in a singular cell.

That means that given the way the Java programming system is designed, there will be no expected dependency from one independent cell to another.

Remember that objects within the Java programming environment are meant to be stand alone, and there are no global variables to reference.

Abstraction

Abstraction simply refers to the process of hiding unnecessary details of an object and only showing the ones that are relevant. **Encapsulation** on the other hand simply means the binding of the states and the methods of an object together.

This binding eventually creates something called a class (we'll cover that in a little bit). Finally, **message passing** refers to the ability of objects to interact with other objects.

High – level programming languages, on the other hand, have a much higher level of abstraction, meaning that code goes through a program called a compiler, which acts as the computer's translator, before the computer is able to use it.

This level of abstraction is usually to the point where the programming language already has syntax similar to English, a global language.

The compiler assumes the role of the translator between the high – level language and the machine.

This allows the programmer to write their program in a more natural manner, as it allows for the coder to use more "natural" language, and the higher – level language allows for some functions to be automated, making life much easier for the coder.

The trade – off here however is that the code has to go through a compiler, which will take lengthier for the program to run and execute, and the computer will often use more memory as compared to a lower – level language. Amongst these high – level languages are the more frequently – known ones, such as Python, C++, and our topic for today, Java.

Chapter 16: Java Interview Questions

The Java Programming Language_

What is the WORA principle? Why is it beneficial?

How can Java applications run on multiple platforms?

What is the difference between the JRE and the JDK?

What is the difference between procedural programming and object-oriented programming?

Object-Oriented Programming (Part I)_

What is the difference between a class and an object?

What happens when an object is instantiated for the first time?

What is the difference between a primitive type and an object?

What is the difference between autoboxing and unboxing?

What is an array?

How is a String different from a regular object?

What is the difference between a StringBuilder and a StringBuffer?

Why are enums superior to String or Integer constants?

What is the difference between package-by-layer and package-by-feature?

Object-Oriented Programming (Part II)

What is the difference between a method declaration and a method signature?

What is a recursive method?

What is the final keyword used for?

What is the static keyword used for?

Why can't a static method access a nonstatic field?

What are access modifiers used for? What are the different types?

What are annotations used for?

The Object Superclass

What is the difference between a shallow copy and a deep copy?

Why is a copy constructor preferable to the clone method?

What is the difference between the identity operator and the equals() method?

What is the relationship between the hashCode() method and the equals() method?

What is the default implementation of the toString() method?

Why is the finalize() method unreliable for cleanup operations?

Composition & Inheritance

What is the difference between composition and inheritance?

What is the difference between method overriding and method overloading?

How would you determine whether to use composition or inheritance?

Abstract Classes & Interfaces_

What is the difference between an abstract class and an interface?

How would you determine whether to use an abstract class or an interface?

Why can't a class be declared both final and abstract?

What is the value of designing a codebase around the use of interfaces?

What are anonymous classes used for?

What is a closure?

What is a lambda expression?

Exceptions

What is an exception?

What is the difference between an unchecked and a checked exception?

How would you determine whether to use an unchecked or a checked exception?

How does a try/catch/finally block work?

How does the try-with-resources statement work?

Generics

What is the difference between a compile-time error and a runtime error?

What is the purpose of generics?

What are the different types of generic wildcards?

What is type erasure?

What are some of the limitations of generics?

Concurrency

What is the lifecycle of a Thread?

Why is synchronization necessary on shared resources?

What is used as a lock for synchronized static and synchronized non-static methods?

What would happen if two different threads hit two synchronized non-static methods on the same object simultaneously?

What would happen if two different threads hit a synchronized static method and synchronized non-static method on the same object simultaneously?

What one thing does the volatile keyword guarantee about a variable?

What two things does the synchronize keyword guarantee about a block of code?

What are some built-in concurrent data structures?

What is the executor framework?

What is a ThreadLocal variable?

What are atomic variables?

Memory Management

How does the JVM divide memory on the heap?

What is the standard algorithm for garbage collection?

What are memory leaks? How can they be identified?

What are the four different types of references?

What is a ReferenceQueue?

Why is a phantom reference safer than using the finalize() method?

Java Database Connectivity

What is JDBC?

What are the two ways of acquiring a Connection object?

What is the difference between the three types of Statements?

What is a ResultSet?

What is an SQL injection attack? How can it be prevented?

What are the advantages and disadvantages of object-relational mapping?

What is Hibernate?

Web Applications

What is a servlet container?

What is a web application?

What is a WAR file?

What is a web.xml file?

What is the difference between a Servlet and an HttpServlet?

What is the difference between a Servlet and a JSP?

What is a servlet filter?

What is the model-view-controller pattern?

Web Services

What is service-oriented architecture?

What are web services?

What is the difference between a SOAP web service and a REST web service?

What is the difference between JAX-WS and JAX-RS?

What are some frameworks that aid in the development of Java web services?

Algorithms

What is Big O notation? What are some common examples?

What is a binary search? How well does it perform?

What is insertion sort? How well does it perform?

What is merge sort? How well does it perform?

What is quicksort? How well does it perform?

What is timsort? How well does it perform?

Java Collections Framework

What is the difference between an ArrayList and a LinkedList?

How does a HashMap work internally?

What would happen if a key's hashCode() or equals() method was incorrect?

What is the difference between a stack and a queue?

What is the difference between a binary search tree, red-black tree, and a heap?

What is the difference between a HashSet, LinkedHashSet, and TreeSet?

What is the difference between a fail-fast iterator and a fail-safe iterator?

Streams

What is the Stream API and why is it useful?

What is the difference between intermediate operations and terminal operations?

Why is the order of intermediate operations important?

What is the difference between parallel streams and sequential streams?

Java Time

What is the Java Time-Scale?

What is the difference between a LocalDateTime and a ZonedDateTime?

What is the difference between an Instant, OffsetDateTime, and ZonedDateTime?

What is the difference between a Period and a Duration?

Important Interfaces

What is the Autocloseable interface?

What is the Comparable interface?

What is the Comparator interface?

What is the Iterable interface?

What is the Runnable interface?

What is the Callable interface?

What is the Serializable interface?

What is a functional interface? What are some common functional interfaces?

Creational Design Patterns

What is the builder pattern? When is it useful?

What is the factory pattern? When is it useful?

What is the abstract factory pattern? When is it useful?

What is the prototype pattern? When is it useful?

What is the singleton pattern? When is it useful?

Structural Design Patterns_

What is the adapter pattern? When is it useful?

What is the composite pattern? When is it useful?

What is the decorator pattern? When is it useful?

What is the facade pattern? When is it useful?

What is the flyweight pattern? When is it useful?

Behavioral Design Patterns_

What is the command pattern? When is it useful?

What is the observer pattern? When is it useful?

What is the strategy pattern? When is it useful?

What is the visitor pattern? When is it useful?

What is the null object pattern? When is it useful?

Reflection

What is reflection?

What is type introspection?

What is a Class object?

What is a Field object?

What is a Method object?

What are some of the pros and cons of reflection?

Dependency Injection

What is the inversion of control pattern?

What is the difference between a service locator and dependency injection?

What is the difference between constructor injection and setter injection?

What is the Spring container?

What are the different ways of configuring a Spring container?

What is the lifecycle of a Spring container?

Aspect-Oriented Programming

What is the difference between a core concern and a cross-cutting concern?

What is aspect-oriented programming?

What is the difference between an interface proxy and an inheritance proxy?

What is the difference between runtime weaving and binary weaving?

What is the AspectJ library?

Unit Testing

What is test-driven development? Why is it beneficial?

What is a unit test?

What is JUnit?

What are text fixtures?

What are mock objects?

Programming Problems

How would you write a method that calculates the factorial of a number?

How would you determine whether a string is a palindrome?

Given a line of text, how would you verify that the number of open and closed parentheses are balanced?

Given an unsorted list with one missing number from 1 to 100, how would you determine the missing number?

Personal Questions

Could you tell us about yourself and your experience?

Could you tell us about any side projects you've worked on?

Could you tell us about a time you solved a particularly challenging problem?

Could you tell us about a time you resolved a disagreement with a coworker?

What was your previous development environment like?

Why you are interested in working at our company?

Why you are leaving your previous job?

What is your biggest weakness? What is your biggest strength?

Chapter 17: Java Language and Terminology

Absolute filename

An absolute filename is a filename with a full path that is provided from the top or the root of the file system tree, or example c:\Java\bin\javac.exe

Abstraction

Abstraction is a simple representation of a complex situation. In basic terms, abstraction hides how a section of code or program works and shows only the functionality of it. This is designed to make it easier to maintain, read and work on the code. OOP design often revolves around finding an abstraction level to work with when real-life objects are being modeled. Too high a level and insufficient detail is capture; too low and you run the risk of a program being more complicated to create and difficult to understand that it should be.

Abstract method

An abstract method is a method whose header contains the reserved keyword, abstract. Abstract methods do not have a method body. Any method that has been designed inside an interface is considered abstract, with no exceptions. An abstract method's body is defined inside an abstract class subclass or, if a class implements the interface, within that class.

Abstract Windowing Toolkit

The AWT, or Abstract Windowing Toolkit contains a collection of classes that are designed to make creating applications with GUIs (graphical user interface) much simpler. You will find these in the java.awt group of packages and classes included are for buttons, windows, menus, frames, text areas and more.

Accessor method

An accessor method is a method that has been designed specifically to provide access to a class private attribute. By Java convention, accessor methods are prefixed with get and then the attribute name. For example, to gain access to an attribute called speed, the accessor method would be getSpeed(). When attributes are set as private, it stops objects from external classes from modifying the value unless a mutator method is used. We can use accessor methods to provide specific access to the private attribute values and to stop other objects in other classes from accessing the private attribute – the correct visibility needs to be used for the accessor to achieve this.

Actor

See client.

Actual argument

This is the value of the argument passed from outside a method into a method. When the method is called, the values (actual argument) will be copied to the formal arguments that correspond to it. The actual argument type and the formal argument types must be compatible with one another.

Actual parameter

See actual argument.

Address space

This is the virtual memory area that a process runs in.

Agent

See server.

Aggregation

This is an OOP concept, a type of relationship where one object has at least one other subordinate object making up its state. These subordinate objects don't tend to have an independent existence outside the object that contains them. When this object no longer has a reason to exist, neither do its subordinates. For example, you may have a GasStation object that has a few pump objects. Once the GasStation object is destroyed or has no further use, the pump objects follow suit. Aggregation is also known as a HAS-A relationship, distinguishing form inheritance which is an IS-A relationship.

Aliases

Aliases are several references to one object. The object may receive messages from any of the aliases and any change in state the results from a message will be easily detected by all.

Anonymous array

This is an array that has been created with no identifier. Anonymous arrays tend to be created as actual arguments like this:

// An anonymous array of integers is created

YearlyRainfall y2k = new YearlyRainfall(

new int[]{ 10, 8, 9, 9, 5, 3, 2, 0, 3, 3, 8, 11}

);

Anonymous arrays can also be returned as the result of a method.

Anonymous class

An anonymous class is one that does not have a class name. this type of class is generally a subclass or an interface implementation and normally gets created as an actual argument or is returned as a result of a method. For example:

quitButton.addActionListener(new ActionListener(){

public void actionPerformed(ActionEvent e){

System.exit(0);

  }

});

Anonymous object

An anonymous object is an object that gets created with no identifier. Usually, they are array elements, results of methods or actual arguments. For example:

private Point[] vertices = {

new Point(0,0),

new Point(0,1),

new Point(1,1),

new Point(1,0),

};

Also see anonymous class as, very often, anonymous objects come from anonymous classes

API

See application programming interface.

Append mode

Append mode is a mode of file writing in which the contents of a file are kept when the file gets opened and new content gets appended.

Applet

An applet is a small Java program that is based on the Applet or the JApplet class. Mostly they are used for providing active content on a web page and they have a number of features that set them apart from a standard Java graphical app, including security restrictions that limit them in what they can do and having no main method defined by a user.

Application

Application is sometimes used synonymously for the word program but, as far as Java is concerned, application is the term used to describe GUI programs that aren't applets.

Application programming interface (API)

The API is a set of definitions used for writing a program. In Java, an API is a set of classes, packages and interfaces used for creating complex applications without having to start from the bottom up.

Argument

An argument is the information or data passed to a method. Sometimes arguments are called parameters. If a method expects to be passed arguments the method header must have a declaration for a formal argument for every argument. When the method is called the values for the actual arguments are copied to the formal arguments that correspond with each one.

Arithmetic expression

An arithmetic expression is one that contains numerical values that are of float or int type. For example, the arithmetic operators, like *, +, -, and /, will all take an arithmetic expression as an operand and their results are arithmetic values.

Arithmetic operator

These are a type of operator that will return a numerical result and are part of an arithmetic expression. Operators include +, -, *, /.

Arpanet

Arpanet is the network that came before the global internet.

Array

An array is an object of fixed size that can hold at least zero items of the declared type for the array. For example, an int array will hold int items.

Array initializer

An array initializer is used to initialize an array. It steps in to take the role of the separation creation step and the initialization. For example:

int[] pair = { 4, 2, };

is equivalent to the following four statements.

```
int[] pair;
pair = new int[2];
pair[0] = 4;
pair[1] = 2;
```

Assembler

An assembler is a program that is used for translating programs that are written in the assembly language into a binary form of a specified instruction set.

Assembly language

The assembly language is a symbolic one that corresponds very closely to a central processing unit (CPU) instruction set. The assembler (above) is the translation program that transforms the program into binary.

Assignment operator

The assignment operator is an equal sign (=) used for storing an expression's value into a variable; for example, variable = expression. The right side of the operator must be evaluated before the assignment can be made. An assignment may, on its own be used on an expression. This example assignment statement will store a value of zero into both of the variables – x = y = 0.

Assignment statement

An assignment statement is a statement that contains the assignment operator.

Attribute

An attribute is a specific use of an instance variable. The attribute values in one class instance are defining the current state of that specific instance. Class definitions can impose constraints on the valid instance states through a requirement that a given attribute or attributes do not take particular values. For example, if an attribute holds exam results for a class, it should not have negative values. An attribute may be manipulated using mutator and accessor methods.

Base case

A base case is a non-recursive route taken through a recursive method

Base type

The base type indicates the item type in an array, i.e. the arrays' defined type. For example:

int[] numbers;

Numbers have a base type of int. If the base case is the type of class, it will be indicating lowest supertype of the objects that the array can store. For example:

Ship[] berths;

All that can be stored in berths are instances of the class called Ship. If an array's base type is Object, it may be used for storing instances for any class.

Behavior

Class methods are what implement the behavior of a class. The behavior of a specific object is a mixture of the class method definitions and the current state of the specific object.

Big-endian

A type of machine. One of the most common differences between machines is how they store each byte of numerical data with many bytes. A big-endian machine will store high-order bytes first, followed by low-order bytes.

Also see little-endian

binary

A binary is base 2 number representation. With base 2 only 1 and 1 are used as digits and the positions of the digits are representing successive powers of 2.

Also see bit

Binary operator

A binary operator is an operator that will take two operands. Java has several binary operators, including some of the arithmetic and Boolean operators.

Binary search

A binary search is a search that looks through sorted data where the central position is looked at first. The search will then go to the left or the right, eliminating the other side of the data space. This is repeated for each step until all the data has been searched or the specific item has been located.

Bit

A bit is a binary digit. It can take only two values, 0 and 1. A bit is a basic block for building both data and programs. A computer will move data around on a regular basis in multiples of units made up of 8 bits, generally called bytes

Bit manipulation operator

A bit manipulation operator, like |, &, and ∧, are used for manipulating bits inside data item bytes. The <<, >> and >>> shift operators are bit manipulation operators too.

Blank final variable

A blank final variable is a final variable that wasn't initialized when it was declared. These variables need to be initialized in one of two ways before it can be used – in every class constructor or in an instance initialization block.

Block

A block is a section of code made up of declarations and statements enclosed in a pair of opening and closing curly brackets {}. Both a class body and a method body are blocks. Blocks are also used for enclosing nested scope levels.

Bookmark

A bookmark is used by a web browser as a way of remembering URL details.

Boolean

a Boolean is a primitive data type in Java. It has just two possible values – TRUE or FALSE.

Boolean expression

a boolean expression is one that results in a boolean, i.e. TRUE or FALSE. The && and the | operators, among others, will take a boolean operand, producing a boolean result. Relational operators will take operands of different types and will also produce a boolean result.

Boot

A computer "boots" up when you turn it on and the term is derived from the phrase "pulling yourself up by your bootstraps". When a computer is first switched on it must load everything it needs from its disks before it can be used but, to do this, there is a program it needs and this is called a bootstrap.

Bootstrap classes

A bootstrap class is part of the Java Platform Core API, like those from the java.io and java.lang packages.

Boundary error

A boundary error is one that happens as a result of a mistake happening at the edge of a problem, such as no items of data, indexing off an array edge, a loop termination and more. Boundary errors are very common logical errors.

Bounded repetition

Bounded repetition is where statements in the body of a loop get performed a certain number of times – the number of times is worked out when the loop begins. Java does not have any control structure that will guarantee bounded repetition.

Also see unbounded repetition

Bounds

A bound is the limit of a collection or array. In Java, a lower limit will always be zero and, where arrays are concerned, an upper bound will always be one less than the array length and it is fixed. When you index outside a collection or array bound, you will get an IndexOutOfBoundsException thrown.

Branch instruction

A branch instruction will store an instruction address in the counter for a program. The result is that the next instruction fetched may not be the one that immediately follows the branch instruction and this causes disruption in the normal sequence of instruction execution. The result of this is conditional instruction execution and repetition.

Break statement

A break statement is a statement for breaking out of a loop, a labeled block or a switch statement. In every case, control flow moves to the statement that immediately follows the block containing the statement.

Bridging method

A bridging method is one that provides a bridge between methods in a public interface for a class and the private implementation of that interface. Usually, bridging methods are non-public in terms of visibility.

Byte

A byte is, in computing terms, eight data bits. In Java, it is also a primitive data type with a size of eight bits.

Bytecode

The Java compiler translates Java source files into bytecode which is the instruction set of the JVM. All bytecode is stored in a .class file.

CONCLUSION

I would like to thank you for choosing my guide on Java programming.

As you can see, it is a simple yet complex language, with so many different aspects to learn. By now you should have a good understanding of the core concepts of Java programming and how to use it.

Your next step is, quite simply, practice.

And keep on practicing. You cannot possibly read this guide once and think that you know it all.

I urge you to take your time going through this; follow the tutorials carefully and don't move on from any section until you fully understand it and what it all means.

To help you out, there are several useful Java forums to be found online, full of people ready and willing to help you out and point you in the right direction.There are also loads of online courses, some free and some that you need to pay for, but all of them are useful and can help you take your learning to the next level.

Did you enjoy this guide? I hope that it was all you wanted and more and it has put you on the right path to getting your dream job!

C PROGRAMMING LANGUAGE FOR BEGINNERS

A step by step guide to learn C programming and series

Will Norton

Introduction

Programming has changed the world and is still ruling the technological industry with wonders achieved that is often difficult to imagine. Efficient programmers are scarce and industries are looking out for fresh talent. A lot of programmers in the initial stage of the technological revolution depended on badly written structured programming languages such as Pascal, Haskel, Cobalt etc.

They have serious issues with the syntactical structure and the way they define things. At this point, C has emerged as a logical and effective programming language that can achieve what it intended to. A lot of programmers at first found it very different from other languages they have learned. But as time passed on C has become programmers favorite and is still one of the most popular and beginners intended programming languages despite competition from other high-level programming languages such as Java and Python.

Even now, if you have any programming background from other traditional programming languages such as Java and Python, you will find it extremely hard to understand the essence of language and create complex programs by yourself in C language. A lot of beginners find C as an old programming language that is outdated now. However, it is false and C programming language is still a popular and important language to be learned if you are dealing with system programming use-cases such as compilers and embedded systems.

What will you learn from this book?

As mentioned beforehand, this book is a layman's introduction to the C programming language with the help of well-curated examples chosen by the book author. This book explains all the basic programming concepts in a much easier way to understand for beginners.

We hope that his book will serve as a good learning experience and a trigger to enjoy programming for our readers.

How to use this book?

Programming books are often theoretical and may make readers deviate easily. This is the reason why we wrote these simple programming books that will let you understand the topics in an easy way.

All we ask you is to enjoy the process of programming.

Use a compiler to practice all of the mentioned code in this book. Programming is best learned when you try to do things.

There a lot of books that teach C programming language in the market. Thanks for choosing to let you enlighten the importance of C language.

Let us start!

Chapter 1: What is the C language?

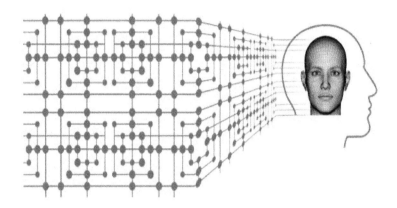

This book is a comprehensive introduction to C language with in-depth examples. It is often misunderstood that C has lost its popularity due to the entrance of modern programming languages such as Java and Python.

However, a lot of beginners don't understand that C is still extensively used to develop compilers and operating systems.

A lot of advanced programming concepts used in C language are still considered a pathway to understanding programming in a better way.

This chapter introduces various important characteristics of C language in detail. We recommend you to use an operating system of your choice to experiment with the programs introduced in this book.

Let us go!

History of C

It is mandatory to discuss the history of a programming language before starting to discuss its specific components, principles, and philosophy. In the 1970s when the programming industry was very small and when there were very few effective programming languages, C was invented in the Bell labs by Denis Ritchie. He developed C language to use it for the development of the UNIX operating system that Bell labs corporation is trying to build. Almost all the components of the UNIX system are extensively written using the C programming language. A lot of graphical user functionalities were also implemented with the help of the C language.

Luckily, UNIX has become very popular in the technological landscape and has given C its required popularity. With the initial success of C language, Denis Ritchie and Bell labs started to distribute C language within different operating systems. One of the famous operating systems that came equipped with C language in the old times is IBM PC. A lot of the computer-related industries started to implement their code while developing C programming applications. So, within a very little time, C has evolved into one of the most popular middle-level languages.

Even after 50 years after its invention, C is still considered one of the most important middle-level languages that the world has ever seen. It is still widely used to develop system programming applications and artificial intelligence applications that deal with hardware equipment such as Robotics and Electric cars.

Why is it so special?

First of all, understand that C language is considered bad for developing modern web and mobile applications.

There are several modern programming languages such as Java, Php to serve this purpose.

C language programming is exclusively used in real-world system applications where we need to work with the hardware at a low level.

Modern programming languages have very fewer libraries for this sort of implementation and practically very bad programmatical structure that can make them nearly impossible to effectively interact with the lower-level components of the hardware.

Whereas, C can interact with hardware components very effectively due to the syntactical structure and programmatical process flows it follows. This is the reason why still C is considered best to create new operating systems and compilers.

Features of C language

Even though C deals with low-level hardware resources it is often considered as a middle-level language because it integrates itself with various high-level programming language capabilities such as neat syntax and organizing structures.

C language is also known widely because it is used as an entry-level teaching resource in various universities such as Harvard, Stanford, and Princeton, etc.,

At the initial stages of the development of C language, it has become difficult for programmers to develop systematic updates for the programming language due to a lot of companies creating different libraries and features that can be added to the language. Due to this reason, International standard organization (ISO) started to declare individual library functions for the C programming language.

All the programmers are suggested to use this respective format for better results. You can find out the latest guidelines from the official C language website.

Here are some of the essential features of the C language:

1) Portable

C language is considered extremely portable and can be executed in any operating system. Previously, it is developed to be run on MS-DOS systems. But with the explosion of windows, Mac and Linux operating systems C has expanded its ability to support different operating systems. A lot of third-party software developers also have developed tens of compilers to run C language programs effectively.

2) Light

C language is often considered lighter than the other high-level programming languages that have occupied the mainstream industry today. Even C++, the successor of C language implements more lines of code than the C. The reason for the lightweight features of C is due to its effective syntax principles. A lot of modern programming languages such as Java, Scala are forced to use complex boiler code syntax to run applications on various platforms. C, on the other hand, uses simple and strict syntax that makes the language a light-weight programming entity.

3)Functional programming

The most important difference between C and other high-level languages is that it supports functional programming. It uses procedures to complete a task in a repetitive mode. Other high-level languages use the object-oriented paradigm to implement different features in the software. Functional programming is often considered effective to develop system-level applications.

However, with the latest updates, we can also implement the object-oriented paradigm in C language. After thorough checks we have done we are not completely satisfied with the object-oriented programming features that C language offers. We recommend you to learn Python or Java if you are keen to develop applications in the object-oriented paradigm. If you are comfortable with a simple, effective paradigm then we suggest you try procedural programming that C provides.

4) Extensible

One of the important features of the C language is that it can be expanded accordingly to utilize our purposes. A lot of space communication facilities such as NASA use this functionality to develop their libraries that can be used to interact with their hardware machines and rockets. This advantage of adding our own functions to the default library is very useful when you are developing your operating systems that are similar to Windows or Mac.

5)Usage of pointers

A pointer is an advanced feature that is available in C language to point out the hardware value of a variable. Pointers can be used to point to a memory location and can be used in the logical implementation of complex features in the program. Very few programming languages use pointers to represent storage location values. Even though having its disadvantages pointers are still a valuable source of resource to implement complex features in the software systems.

6)Huge library of functions

C provides a large library of system functions. All these functions serve a purpose and can be used for developing high-level system applications. We will be discussing different time functions and string manipulation functions in detail in the later chapters of this book.

Apart from these features, C language is also an open-source resource and is free to use.

With this, we have completed a brief and thorough introduction to the C language.

This chapter acts as an introduction to C language by experts' words.

In the next chapter, which is a continuation of the concepts explained here we will discuss various advantages and applications of C language in detail.

Let us go!

Chapter 2: Why C language is important?

The previous chapter is an ode to the importance and history of the C programming language in a comprehensive manner.

This chapter further expands the concepts that the previous chapter has introduced. We will in detail discuss different C versions that are available along with the applications and advantages of C programing language in detail.

This is a theoretical chapter that helps to place some pretty basic ideas in your mind which can help you when you are dealing with complex programming problems.

Follow along to know more about it!

Why is the C programming language important?

There are a lot of programming languages nowadays and all of them serve a significant purpose. This section of the chapter explains some of the reasonable arguments that prove that C language is better than those high-level modern programming languages. However, it is the programmer's own choice to choose the language that he is most comfortable with.

We are not denying that fact. We are just giving pretty basic arguments that prove that C language is the best for certain applications and mediums.

a) They are fast

The important advantage of C is it can deal directly with hardware resources. This advantage over other high-level languages makes C a fast processing language. A lot of other programming languages offer abundant extra features but they cannot beat the faster processing time that C offers.

b) It is portable

Portability is one of the main reasons for the initial success of C. Back in those days, assembly languages have made portability a distant difficulty and often forced programmers to create multiple versions of code to deploy on different devices. However, C started to offer advanced portability customizations that can help us run the program code on any platform with the help of a supportive compiler. You need not worry about your software not running on different operating systems anyone by using C as your primary development language.

c) Modularity

C language offers you to store the snippets of your code in the form of modular entities. These are like user made functions that can be imported whenever they are needed. These are more related to packages in Java programming language. Modularity's are extensible and can solve a lot of problems that programmers are facing.

d) A statically typed language

There is a lot of argument in programming circles between static and dynamic typed languages related to which is effective. The difference between dynamic and statically typed languages is that during compile time, statically typed languages show errors in a much faster significance. C is a statically typed language and performs at a faster rate due to this feature. However, we don't deny the fact that dynamically typed languages provide much better security features during the compilation process.

e) A learning resource

C language apart from holding a lot of advantages can help you understand programming in depth. A lot of modern programming languages are dynamic and will not provide you a way to learn and adapt the programming philosophy that paved a path for a technological revolution. However, C, on the other hand, provides a lot of significant information that can help you understand the working process of computers and programming.

This is the sole reason why C is extensively used as a primary programming language for various graduate courses in topmost universities.

f) Important to understand other languages

C is a learning pathway to understand different programming languages such as Python, C++, and C#. A lot of compilers, interpreters and IDE's of these famous programming languages are developed using C. Learning about C can help you understand the programmatical syntax structure of other high-level languages.

In the next section, we will in detail discuss some of the applications of the C programming language.

Follow along!

Applications of the C programming language

As said before, C is a system-level language that can be extensively used to develop system-level applications. Here are some of them.

a) To develop compilers

A lot of compiler technologies are built upon C. Compilers are an essential component that is necessary to run a software or an application. Also, compilers are required to understand the hardware architecture before compiling the program.

This is the reason why C programming language is highly adaptable for developing compilers and its add-on applications.

It can also be used to develop interpreters and assemblers.

b) To create operating systems

Operating systems are an easy interface that serves as a mediator between the user and the computer. A lot of operating systems use C as a primary language due to its extensibility and fast processing nature. Linux, a famous open-source operating system used C to develop its most important component kernel.

c) System-based applications

A lot of devices/applications that are linked with hardware resources use C to develop applications. For example, Tesla cars use C language to communicate between its components. Robotics, a future technology also focuses on much about complex C programming concepts.

What are some downsides?

Like other programming languages, C is also not perfect in some cases. This section is provided for you to understand what C cannot offer for the programmers.

a) It Doesn't support object-oriented paradigm

All of the programmers knew that the Object-oriented programming paradigm is one of the most important and widely used programming paradigms. However, C doesn't support OOP's and solely focuses on procedural programming with the help of functions. A lot of institutions, services use packaging structure to distribute files between their employees. So, due to the procedural nature of the C programming language, it is often not considered as a primary development language for projects that require a huge number of contributors.

b) Not everything can be done with C

C is not a multi-use language. It cannot be useful for web and mobile application development, unlike other high-level programming languages. For example, Java can be used to develop desktop, mobile and web applications. C is not a multi-purpose programming language but a programming language that serves its work best.

In the next section, we will discuss the available versions of the C programming language.

We will also provide a small tutorial to help you download the executable file of C language to install C dependencies and compiler in your system.

Follow along!

Versions of C

C language is usually available in 2 versions as explained below.

a) ANSI C

This is the old version of the C programming language that is used in Bell Labs to develop the UNIX operating system. This is often considered complex to learn and deal with.

You can download and install it from the official C language website.

b) ISO C

This is the modern C language package that is often used to create multi-purpose programming applications. It is extensible and light-weight. You can directly download it from the official website to start using it.

Installing C in Windows

Step 1:

Programmers usually use the GCC compiler to create C programming applications. To install the GCC compiler you need to first download few dependencies that are necessary to install it. First of all, download Cygwin from its official website. Install it in the default folder of your choice. Carefully download the correct version of Cygwin that is compatible with your windows operating system.

Step 2;

After installing Cygwin, you need to download GCC packages from its applications. These are essential to run the GCC compiler

Step 3:

In the last step, download the GCC compiler and change the environment variables to make the compiler work without any flaws. We recommend you to constantly update the compiler for accessing latest features

Installation in Linux:

To install a C compiler in Linux you need to use the pip package manager.

Here is the format:

pip install GCC

After downloading the GCC compiler, Linux kernel will check for the dependencies and will automatically download all of those resources for you. You can use the vim text editor to create code and save them to execute in the terminal interface.

Use the same procedure as windows, to download the GCC compiler for Mac operating system.

You can also download several IDE's and install them to use them with fewer memory resources. A lot of this software is available for all the famous operating systems.

With this, we have completed a brief introduction to the advantage of the C programming language. In the next chapter, we will start learning about the importance of the program in detail. Follow along!

Chapter 3: What is a Program?

From the 1950s computers have slowly occupied and lead the technological revolution. At the initial stages, it is considered extremely difficult to just do numerical calculations using first-generation computers.

Magnetic cards are used as input and output devices and they almost occupied a whole room. However, with time computer scientists have made this problem go away. Nowadays, we can find computers in the size of wrists with gigabytes of memory.

The success of computers is mainly due to programs that are used to make software.

Programming languages are developed to create meaningful programs. In this chapter, we will in detail discuss the importance of programs and how they work.

Let us go!

What is programming?

Computers are a lot different from humans.

They are not neurally active and doesn't consist of any emotions that humans possess. Computers mostly rely on instructions.

The only reason why computers have become better than humans is that they do tasks effectively without wasting any time. However, we can consider computers as dumb machines. If they are not provided with a solution to the problem beforehand, they can't solve it. Even after twenty years of tremendous research robotics is not a successful field because it is difficult to make machines that take decisions by themselves.

In the early stages of computer development, people used to use instruction sets to complete tasks. These instructions sets are allowed to use only for scientific and military purposes.

Several multinational companies started to experiment with their employees to create a whole new way to pass instructions to computers. All dreamt of an easy way to make things work out.

After a few years with great research, computer scientists introduced the concept of programming to the technological world with the help of programming languages. Programming languages provide a set of defined libraries that can help you to create programs.

Programs are considered as an analytical representation of algorithms and the definite task of creating valid programs that can be understood by a machine is known as programming.

In the next section, we will start discussing a program on a much deeper level.

What is a Program?

Programming languages use Programs to give varied instructions to the computing machines. From a mathematical perspective, the process of giving step-by-step instructions is called an algorithm.

A lot of statistical concepts in mathematics too use algorithms to solve a problem. An algorithm is not only a step-by-step procedure but a way that is proven to be effective.

In programming, we use programs to create a logical instruction that can make us solve a specific problem as quickly and effectively as possible.

Experienced programmers try to create programs that are in less code length and which consumes fewer resources. It is not only important to create a working code, but it is also important to create code that is feasible and which effectively understands the resources that are available to it.

What is the difference between Algorithm & program?

Algorithm and program are closely interlinked. When a programmer is trying to solve a problem, he first finds a logical and provable way to complete it.

He monitors the inputs and outputs that are available and creates a step-by-step procedure to solve it.

This is called an algorithm from a theoretical basis.

However, computers can't understand human language. They use the binary system to understand instructions.

This is the reason why we need to represent our algorithm in a way such that computers can understand.

This process is technically known as programming. Programming uses a set of programs to make the computer understand what needs to be done.

What are the programming languages?

When the concept of programming is introduced the scientific and computing community has overwhelmed. They started developing a lot of instruction sets and started developing programs with them.

However, just after a few projects programmers and computing scientists understood that there needs to be a specific regular platform to create programs. It is not feasible to use each other's instruction sets to create meaningful software.

So, they worked hard to develop programming languages that can maintain and provide a lot of libraries for their usage. Programming languages like ABC, Pascal are developed and people started using them for developing programs. All these distinct programming libraries are enhanced and named as programming languages. They are also called as high-level languages and remember that they are only used to make it easy for humans to communicate with computers.

We always need a compiler to let computers understand the program.

You will learn about the programming process in detail in the next chapter.

How programs can be written?

Programs are usually written in an operating system. For example, Windows is an operating system. Traditionally programmers used to use a text editor and command-line tools to write and run a program. But nowadays, a lot of programmers use IDE (Integrated development environments) to develop and debug programs. If you are working for an open-source project then you must have good knowledge about Git-based programs such as GitHub to access and contribute to the projects.

Here are some of the tools that can be used to develop C programming applications.

1) NetBeans IDE

NetBeans is a famous IDE that is often used by C language programmers to develop console applications. It has a good supportive development team that updates relevant features once in a while.

Compile-time is also very smooth and can help you create large applications with less RAM.

2) Code blocks

Code blocks is a multi-purpose ide that can be used to create programming applications. It is commonly used to develop C++ programs. However, you can use a simple tweak to start developing C language applications using it.

C programming provides a smart coding facility where you can easily highlight the relevant code.

3) Sublime text

Sublime text is not a usual IDE but a beautiful text editor that provides a lot of plugins to improve your productivity while programming. It also looks beautiful and is available in both free and premium versions.

4) Eclipse

Eclipse is an Integrated development environment that is usually used to develop java applications and android apps. However, Eclipse is also well versed with C addons to develop complex applications.

We recommend you to try Eclipse if you are trying to develop compiler software with C. Eclipse provides a linter to constantly check C syntax.

With this, we have completed a chapter that explains in-depth about a program.

In the next chapter, we will use certain programming concepts to understand the programming process.

Let us dive into it!

Chapter 4: What is a Programming process?

To understand C programming in depth it is important to learn about the default programming process in detail. Just like every other technological advancement, programming languages too follow a strictly adhered guideline system to make things work in the way they are intended to. In the previous chapter, we discussed in detail the basic structure of a program.

In this chapter, we will help you to understand the basic process of programming languages and programs itself.

This is a theoretical chapter and will introduce some of the historical concepts related to programming to make you aware of various instances.

Let us go!

In the previous chapter, we got a good layman understanding of the program. Programs are used to make computers understand what we are saying.

As said before, it is difficult to make computers understand the programs by themselves. So, computer scientists started to create programs that can be compiled and converted into machine language.

All the programs are compiled, interpreted before running the program.

This task is done by interpreters and compilers.

In the next section, we will talk about the programming process that happens when a program is compiled.

Programming process

Before trying to knowing about the complete programming process it is essential to know about assembly languages. Assembly languages are used extensively before the invention of programming languages.

Assembly languages provided programmers to deal with computers on a higher level. Before assembly languages, computer programmers used to remember binary sequences to complete very simple tasks. Even for a simple multiplication, it used to take minutes for the first-generation computers. Tedious, isn't it?

However, with the entrance of assembly languages, things became better. Assembly languages use a certain defined location or defined names to perform operations. So, to create applications programmers used to create assembled code which can be understood by an assembler to provide results. Eventually, though usage of assembly languages became troublesome for the programmers.

The failure of assembly languages is considered mostly because of its non-portability.

The assembled programming code can be only run in the machines that support the instruction set.

After the development of FORTRAN programmers understood the powerful capabilities that programming languages possess. Programming languages are machine-dependent and can be run on any system.

All we need to have is a compiler that can understand and interpret the instructions we are giving.

In the next section, we will in detail discuss the working procedure and philosophy of compilers.

What is a Compiler?

A compiler is a piece of computing component that lexically analyzes the programming code you have written and analyzes it to provide results.

Compilers are essential to run the programs that are created.

Compilers will also help you to understand the syntactical errors that you have performed.

What are the essentials to be remembered?

1) Always remember that the file name is necessary to help your compilers understand whether they are dealing with the right file or not. C++ compilers cannot understand C programming code and vice versa. Compilers are complex software programs that only work with the programming languages they are intended to work upon.

For example, you can't create iOS applications using Eclipse because Eclipse cannot compile iOS applications.

For, a C Program remember that files should consist of .C file format.

You can use a text editor such as vi text editor or sublime text editor to create program files.

2) The compilation process is started or enabled using a set of instructions. Command-line tools use certain syntactical commands to start the compilation process whereas Integrate development environments such as NetBeans use graphical user interfaces to start the compilation process.

Here is the format for the command line:

GCC sample.c

When this particular format is entered in the command line the compilation process will initiate and will show the results if there are no errors. If there are errors, they will be displayed along with the line number.

Process of compiling programs

The compilation is a complex process and involves different stages.

The compilation procedure will not continue further if it deals with any errors or warnings in the process.

Let us take a look into it.

Stage 1: Checking semantic nature

In the first stage, compilers check every component of the program using top to down basis. It checks whether or not the component is following the lexical syntax of the programming language. If everything is right the programming process will proceed to the next stage. However, if errors are encountered due to wrong syntactical structures such as wrong parenthesis statements or missing braces the program will abort and the compilation errors with possible reasons will be displayed on the screen.

Step 2: To assembly language instructions

In this stage, all the processed programming code will be analyzed and converted into assembly language code to be understood by the computing machine. All compilers provide different instruction sets to make this procedure complete fastly. This procedure is essential because an assembler is the only component taht is authorized to convert programming syntax into object code.

Step 3: Linking the object code

In the previous stage of the compilation process, we have generated an object code that can be understood by any computer. In this stage, we need to link the generated object code to any programs that are necessary to run the program. For example, consider packages and libraries that are essential to run the software. Linkage of programs is also known as building. When the object codes are linked you can obtain an executable file that can be opened to run the program. However, a lot of compilers automatically display this executable file as a result.

Step 4: Loading the program

In the last stage, all we need to do is enter the syntactical format that can help us run the program on the screen. For the C programming language, you need to enter a.out to run the program.

What happens after the compilation?

After the compilation process is completed the output will be displayed. If there are any instances where the input values should be entered the program will stop executing and will wait for the input values.

Programs will also respond to events such as mouse clicks. You can also use the debugging feature provided to change any lines of the code and execute the program all over again.

With this, we have completed a brief chapter that explains the programming process that is involved when a program is compiled.

In the next chapter, we will write our first C program and introduce a lot of essential and basic C concepts.

Follow along!

Chapter 5: Writing your first C program

Programming is learned in a better way when combined with examples that explain the syntax structure and process control that the programming language uses.

This chapter is a comprehensive one where we provide a C language example and explore the components of it in detail. Remember that, a lot of the concepts explained in this chapter will be further discussed in detail in the later chapters of this book.

For now, understand the specifics of C programming language with an example.

Follow along!

First C program

```
#include<stdio.h>
// Here, you should enter the main program
int (main {Enter the argument here})
{
  printf( " Christmas is coming soon')
// You can enter the return keyword here if needed
  return value;
}
```

Now, in this section, we will explain about the different components that are mentioned in detail.

Note: Remember that in C language there is no difference between upper- and lower-case letters. Also, whitespaces are allowed and you can start the program from any position on the line. However, it is recommended to follow design guidelines to create a readable programming code. Always follow the guidelines that are designated by the International standards organization (ISO).

1) #include <stdio.h>

This is an easy way to import a library and use the functions that are present in it in the program. It is mandatory to include <stdio.h> in every C program because it imports the major input and output functions such as printf and scanf. This is the format you need to use whenever you import a library to be used on the program code.

For example, #include <math.h> imports all the system math functions and #include<time.h> includes all the system time functions. These are also called as preprocessors in the programming terminology.

2) int main(void)

Here, the main is the program execution point that is often considered as an initial point for compilers. When a C program is compiled, the compiler first checks the code that is present between the braces of the main function. Here int represents the return type it is accustomed to. Also, remember that the void represents that the main function has no parameters. It is important to follow the instructions so that you won't mess up any logical code in the main function.

3) printf(" Christmas is coming soon')

Here printf is the system output function that can print out the values that are present in between the quotation marks on your screen. You can also use scanf to scan the input values. These are called input and output statements in the C programming language. When the program is compiled " Christmas is coming soon" will be displayed on the screen as an output.

4) return value

This is a statement that describes the return value that the main function produces. Usually, it is void or sometimes present in the null format. Return is an important functionality provided by the C programming language that can help us to maintain the resources effectively.

With this, we have explained in detail all the important components that are present in the first program we have discussed.

Compiling and Running the program

In this section, we will talk about the compilation commands for any C language file.

We will also provide instructions to help you run a program without any runtime errors.

Compiling a program

It is important to remember the file name and use the following format in the command line.

Always, make sure that you are in the same directory in the terminal as of the file location

$ GCC {Name of the program file}

When this format is entered on the terminal, it will take some time to compile the program. If there are no errors shown then the program is said to be compiled successfully.

However, if errors occur then you can't run the program unless they are cleared off.

Errors are usually displayed with the line number for easier understanding.

The program will not proceed further unless the errors or cleared off.

Running a Program

After compiling the program, it is now time to run the program using the command-line instructions.

Advanced programming environments such as NetBeans automatically run the programs after compilation is completed.

However, in the command-line interface, you need to enter the following command for running the program.

a.out

After entering the following command your program is completely ready to be run by the command-line interface. You can now enter your program name to display the result.

Here is the command:

$example.c

Here is the output:

Christmas is coming soon

Comments

In the above example program, you might have observed some of the remarks in the program followed by the "//" symbol. These are called comments in a programming language.

Comments are usually used to help programmers who are working in big projects to understand the declaration of variables and the logical algorithms used.

Comments are also an easy way to maintain coherence between the programmers involving in the programming project.

Comments are often considered as a good programming practice and we suggest you use comments while writing your programming code in C language.

C programming language usually provides two types of comments:

a) //

These comments are usually used in the middle of the programs. They are used for providing remarks for the program.

Function and variable declaration are the most common places where these comments (also called as single-line comments) are used.

b)/*.... */

These are called as multi-line comments and are often used at the beginning or end of the programs.

They are used to provide a detail explanation about the programming logic that has been used while writing the program.

They are also used at the beginning of the programs to explain the system libraries or third-party that have been imported for a particular program

For example, a lot of machine learning algorithms developed using C provides a detailed algorithm explanation to the program in the form of multi-line comments.

Variables

Variables are a way to store values and use them repeatedly whenever needed. We will in detail explain variables in the further chapters. But for now, it is recommended to watch out this example to help you understand how variables are declared in the C language.

For now, do not worry about the syntax because we will deal with in detail in the upcoming chapters of this book.

Here is the programming code:

```
#include<math.h>
main()
{
   variable1 = 23;
   variable2 = 45;
   variable3 = variable1+variable2;
    printf(" Print first number as %i/n",variable1)
    printf(" Print first number as %i/n",variable2)
    printf(" Print first number as %i/n",variable3)
}
```

The output will be :

Print first number as 23

Print second number as 45

Print third number as 68

Explanation:

In this program variable1, variable2 and variable 3 are programs that can store a value. The C programming language automatically determines that it is an integer value while taking the input. However, while displaying the print statement you might have observed that it requires parameters. %n is used to declare an integer output statement.

Here we have used assignment operators to declare variables and arithmetic operators to combine or add variables.

In the next chapters, we will discuss important C operations in detail.

New lines

In the previous program, you might have observed '/n' in the programming code. This is usually used to print a new line in the result.

Here is a program:

```
#include<math.h>
main()
{
    variable1 = 67;
    variable2 = 78;
    variable3 = variable1+variable2;
    printf(" Print first number as %i/n /n %i /n ...................
",variable1)
}
```

The result will be:

Print first number as 67

67

....

With this, we have completed a brief introduction to the first C program written in this book.

In the next chapters, we will start an in-depth discussion about various important C programming language concepts.

Let us go!

Chapter 6: Functions

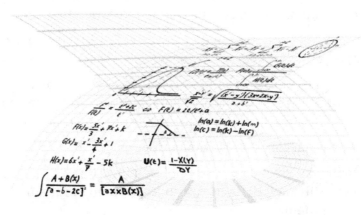

C is a procedural programming language that adversely uses functions to complete tasks. Unlike modern programming languages such as Java which uses classes and objects to create instances, you need to use functions to create varied instances.

Functions are usually determined as reusable code.

They are first implemented for using mathematical calculations in the 13th century.

In this chapter, we will in detail describe functions in the C programming language. We suggest you create your own programs to better understand functions.

Let us go!

What is a function?

Functions are generally used in the mathematical operations to repeat a calculation or set of expressions. Computer programming languages adopted these functional concepts to create and maintain certain defined instructions.

A lot of programming languages provide libraries that can be imported when they want to be used.

For example, in C programming language to use printf and scanf notations you need to import studio.h. This is because printf and scanf are standard input, output functions.

These are also called as system functions.

You can also use your own defined functions which are programmatically known as user-defined functions by importing them.

From a programming perspective, the function is a collection of logical and lexically correct statements that can be used for developing applications. Also, it is important to say that it is mandatory to have at least one function in the program.

Main is the default function.

Why functions are used?

Imagine programming with a lot of static code that does the same task. It is not feasible and consumes a lot of time for the programmers.

This is the reason why functions are used to regulate the large code and maintain equity in the program.

With the help of functions, we can divide the code into many modules and can easily check them with any available debugger. Functions are also to organize and maintain, unlike complex static code that can go on for an infinite distance.

For example, if you want to create a stock investor program in the normal programming instance you need to create static input and output for every option that is displayed on the interface.

However, in procedural programming with the help of functions, you can create options or menu instances that can be used whenever needed.

Advantages of functions

1) Easy

It is easy to maintain and debug the code when functions are present. You can't or it is practically not possible to develop complex code without functions. They are the actual building blocks of the c programming language and will always be. They are easy to create if you understand their basic implementation procedure.

2) Pathway to modules

Modules are an important component in the programming language. They categorize the language and divides or organizes meaningful code in one place. Functions are the basic nature of modules. If you learn about functions you can easily understand the complexity of modules. After learning about higher-order functions in-depth you will understand the importance of modules in a programming language.

3) Debugging

Debugging is a process where the programmers check the programming code continuously and change the affected program code if they find any bugs. Bugs can be used for exploitation purposes by hackers. When effective functions are written it is easy to just change their logic during the debugging process. In this way, we will not encounter any dangerous errors that may compromise the system.

4) Save time

With functions, you will save a lot of time during the programming process. This process is called as code optimization.

Types of functions

Every programming language provides a different type of default system functions. For example, you can use mathematical and time functions in C language from the default libraries. Users can also create functions with new parameters and logical statements.

 These functions are called as user-made functions.

In the next section, we will explain about user-made functions and library functions in detail.

Follow along!

a) library functions

They are already pre-linked with the C compiler that they downloaded.

All the functions are stored in the default c folder and can be imported whenever needed. Printf, scanf are some of the famous predefined functions in the C programming language.

The merits of predefined functions are there is no need to specifically call them during the programming process. Also, they are fast because they are already linked to the compilers. However, remember that they are limited by the functionality they can offer and they cannot be extended by any means.

Also, no one can edit or change the default functions that the C programming provides unlike user made functions.

b) User-made functions

These are the functions that are created by the programmer. For creating functions, you need to follow certain guidelines that the C programming language provides. You need to first define functions and call them whenever needed.

In the next section, we will discuss the function declaration in detail.

Follow along!

How to define a function?

First of all, remember that functions have a unique name and reserved keywords cannot be used as function names.

Here is the format:

Datatype name (//Enter parameters here)

{

  // Enter function logic here

}

Here, a datatype is the return value of the function you are trying to create. For example, if a function returns negative decimal values you need to declare float variables as the data type.

In the next step, you need to enter a valid function name with parameters.

What is a parameter in the function?

To say in layman terms parameters are similar to variables but for functions. Each of the parameters is individually declared with a data type.

Only variables declared in the parameters can be used in the body of the function. If there are any misspells while creating or calling parameters of the function you will encounter run time errors.

At the last step, you need to create logical expressions and statements in the function body. In the function body, you cannot use variables or literals that are not declared before. So, make sure that all the specifiers are included before you start creating logical operations, conditionals, and loops in the function body.

How to call a function?

A function is useless if it cannot be used. Programming doesn't allow usage of functions just by their names due to various potential errors. You need to follow certain rules to call a function in the C programming language.

Here is the format:

Datatype function (// Enter the parameters here)

sample = function (//Enter the parameters here)

Here, the data type represents the type of return value you are expecting. Sample represents a variable name. A function can be called only if the variables are declared with a global specifier.

In the next section, we will in detail discuss function arguments.

Follow along!

What are the function arguments?

Arguments are the values that functions take in the parameter part of the function. You can create functions without arguments too.

There are some varied differences between functions with arguments and without arguments which we will be discussing now in detail.

Functions with arguments

If a function has arguments there is no need to declare variables again in the function body. When function arguments are declared you need to call the functions with arguments. If certain arguments are not shown while calling a function then it will end up with a syntax error.

For example:

function (int x, int y)

Here is a function with two arguments x and y. Here x and y are both of int data type. If you are calling this function in the middle of the program you need to use the below format.

function (3,4)

If you leave the arguments without any values you will not further proceed with the compilation process.

For example,

function (3)

Output:

The syntax is not complete

Functions without arguments

If functions are not declared or enclosed with arguments, they need to be called using a value or reference.

These functions are especially used while creating complex system learning applications.

They don't consist of any parameters but use variables as a way to expand the logical equivalence to the function statements and expressions.

Call by Value

When call by value argument instance is used you cannot change the parameter value again. T

his functionality is used especially when there is a necessity of using constant literal values in the function body.

Here is a program:

```c
#include<stdio.h>
void sample (float first, float second)
{
 double result;
 result=first;
 first=second;
 second=first;
}
main ()
{
 float first=100, second=200;
 result (first, second); // passing value to function
// This is an example to calling a function using a value
}
```

In this program, the function result is called using the value. This is an easy way to declare functions and use them.

In the next section, we will explain another advanced way to call function.

Call by reference

Usually, when a variable or literal is declared they are stored in a memory location. Memory locations can be used to modify or alternate statements and expressions.

You can easily know about your reference storage value using the pointers in the C programming language.

When some advanced functions are used, it becomes a necessity to call the function values using reference points. The advantage of this feature is function value changes everywhere in the program when a reference pointer is used.

Here is a program:

```
#include<stdio.h>
void sample (float first, float second)
{
 double result;
 result=first;
 first=second;
 second=first;
}
main ()
{
 result (&first, &second); // passing value to function by a reference
// This is an example to calling a function using a reference
}
```

In the above program, we use a function that calls the arguments with the help of reference values. In the next section, we will discuss recursion in detail.

Beginners are encouraged to learn about different system library functions too on their own. In the further chapters, we will discuss various string and time manipulative functions in detail.

For now, let us look at an example that helps you understand the essence of recursive programming in C.

Recursive functions

Recursive functions are used to decrease the code length of the complex problems such as sorting algorithms for an example. Creating a recursive function is difficult because it involves complex logical expressions. However, they are famous and popular in programming circles because they can reduce the load on the programing resources with their faster functional calling abilities.

In layman terms, Recursion is a function that repeats by itself. That is, it uses its own arguments as functional parameters.

Recursive functions are usually used in the creation and implementation of advanced data structures such as trees, graphs, and lists.

For your better understanding of the topic in this chapter, we will implement factorial using a recursive function. Follow along!

Here is the program:

```
// Enter the libraries here
#include <stdio.h>
// Main function logic
main ()
{
  long int variable;
  for (variable=0; variable++;variable>11)
{
   // We only display factorial upto 10 numbers
   /* You can change the variable limit if needed */
   print( %n, factorial)
```

```
  // Enter the return value here
  // Factorial recursive logic begins from here
  long int factorial(//Enter parameters here)
  {
    if (variable == 0 )
       factorail == 0
    else
       factorail = result * (result-1)
  }
  return factorial;
  }
```

Explanation:

In the above program, factorial is calculated by a recursive function that calls by itself. First of all, we create two global variables, result, and factorial in the body of the function. Result is a temporary variable that holds the values during the functional process.

Factorial is a variable that holds the end value and prints on the screen. They both use recursive logic to implement a factorial execution process in this program.

We use a conditional and loop statement constantly to check whether are not the limit of factorial is crossed. If 10 numbers are completed, the function will stop recusing itself.

We also used long, a program specifier for the integer values to allocate sufficient resources during the recursive process.

Exercise:

Try to create a recursive function for checking whether two numbers are prime or not.

Procedural programming in the C language

As said before, C is a procedural programming language that relies completely on functions to complete tasks.

The major advantage of procedural programming is they can be used to create a new set of programs from the old programs.

Object-oriented paradigm inspired programming languages such as Java consist of whole new instances and entities which can be difficult to maintain.

Procedural programming can be completely achieved only when you can use functions, identifiers, and logical expressions combined to create efficient programs. Procedural programming has its demerits too. It is not possible to create a machine learning and artificial intelligence applications with the C programming language because they cannot create automatic functions.

With this, we have completed a brief introduction to functions.

In the next section of this book, we will in depth discuss various advanced C programming features such as arrays, structures, and pointers.

For now, we suggest you look at some of the open-sourced GitHub projects to understand the usage of functions in-depth.

In the immediate next chapter, we will discuss various basic operations C programming language can perform.

Let us go!

Chapter 7: Operations

The previous chapter is a dive into the procedural philosophy of C programming language.

Creating functions and using pre-built system functions is the most important task that the C language does.

In this chapter, we will start discussing different C operators and operations that are essential for creating effective programs.

This chapter is explained from a programmatical perspective and consists of a lot of examples.

We suggest you open a compiler and experiment with the code that we present here.

Always remember that programming can be mastered only with practice.

Let us dive into the world of C programming operations!

What are the operations?

To explain in simple terms, operations are the replica of mathematical expressions in the programming languages. Usually, when we do a mathematical problem, we define constants and use functions to solve them using different mathematical applications.

In the same way, programming languages use different operators to achieve a lexical significance related to the mathematical application.

Mathematical operations

First of all, we will start with simple mathematical operators such as addition and subtraction.

Computing is based upon regular mathematical calculations and is mandatory to make programs work effectively.

To conduct mathematical operations with precision and effectiveness we use programming operators in C language.

a) Addition

The addition is usually done with the help of the '+' operator. Using this operator, you can add two variables or literals. You can also use this operator to join two strings.

Here is an example:

```
#include {The libraries needed]
main()
{
   variable1 = 32;
   variable2 = 12;
   variable3 = variable1 + variable2;
   // This is where we use a '+' operator
   printf(" This is the number %n",variable3)
}
```

Output:

This is the number 44

b) Subtraction

Subtraction is denoted by the operator '-'. Using this operator, you can remove or delete the strings and constants that are present. You can also use this operator for separating packages and libraries.

Here is an example:

```
#include {The libraries needed]
main()
{
```

```
variable1 = 32;
variable2 = 12;
variable3 = variable1 - variable2;
// This is where we use a '-' operator
printf(" This is the number %n",variable3)
}
```

Output:

This is the number 20

c) Multiplication

This is the operator that can be used to multiply the variables and constants that are present. You can use this operator with strings to print continuous results. Multiplication operator is also effective for repetitive tasks. It is represented using the '*' operator.

Here is an example:

```
#include {The libraries needed]
main()
{
  variable1 = 32;
  variable2 = 12;
  variable3 = variable1 * variable2;
  // This is where we use a '*' operator
  printf(" This is the number %n",variable3)
}
```

Output:

This is the number 384

d) Division

This is the operator that is used to divide two variables or constants. It is usually represented by the ' / ' operator. We will also discuss the modulus operator that determines the remainder of the division in the later sections of this chapter.

Here is an example:

```
#include {The libraries needed]
main()
{
  variable1 = 32;
  variable2 = 12;
  variable3 = variable1 / variable2;
  // This is where we use a '/' operator
  printf(" This is the number %n",variable3)
}
```

Output:

This is the number 2

Operator precedence

It is also important to remember that the C programming language favors few operators above other operators. This is to resolve any conflicts or ambiguities in a mathematical expression. Usually, * and / are the highest priority operators followed by + and -.

It is important to remember the concept of operator precedence while dealing with a lot of associative code.

As said before, these are the basic operators that are available in the C programming language. C also offers several assignment and logical operators to help you create complex programs.

In the next section, we will start looking at operators in a much deeper sense.

Assignment operator

The assignment operator is used to declare or initiate any identifiers. For example, variables are initiated using the assignment operator.

Here is the format:

variablename = value;

Here '=' is called the assignment operator.

When an assignment operator is used usually the variable is initiated. The assignment operator can also be used to replace the values. Assignment operators turn statements into mathematical expressions.

They can also be used as mutually exclusive and inclusive statements. Assignment operators can be combined with '+' and '-' to create counter operators such as '+=' '-='.

These operators are usually used in producing logical expressions.

Comparison operators

These are the operators that can be used to produce logical equivalence statements. They can be used to compare to statements and provide an option to choose the programming flow.

These operators will be extensively used to develop conditional and loop statements.

a) Equal to operator (==)

This is the operator that is used to compare whether two statements or identifiers are equal or not.

Here is an example:

variable = 23;

varib = 46 ;

if (varfiable == varib)

printf(" this is good")

else

printf(" This is wrong")

Output:

This is wrong.

b) Not Equal to operator (!=)

This is the operator that is used to compare whether two statements or identifiers are not equal.

Here is an example:

variable = 23;

varib = 46 ;

if (varfiable != varib)

printf(" this is good")

else

printf(" This is wrong")

Output:

This is good

c) Greater than and less than operators

These are the operators that can be used to compare two identifiers based on their values. If the logical statement is correct than the value will be produced as a result.

Here is the program:

variable1> variable2

// This is called greater than operator

variable1< variable2

This is called less than operator

variable <= variable2

This is called less than or equal to operator

variable1 >= variable2

This is called greater than or equal to operator

Modulus operator

The modulus operator is considered to be one of the essential operators for programming languages. It just prints out the remainder as the result. However, this mathematical application can be used to regulate system expressions and develop effective system applications.

For example:

if (Var1 % var2)

printf(" This is great")

Logical operators

C language also provides logical operators to compare two statements from a purely logical perspective.

The famous logical operators are AND, OR and NOT.

We will explain them in detail in the next section. Follow along!

a) AND operator

This logical operator displays the result only when both the statements that are involved are true. If any one of them is not true then the program will not execute.

Here is the program code:

```
#include<math.h>
//This is used to import mathematical functions
main()
{
    int a=3;
```

```
int b=6;
int c= a*b;
if( a == 3 AND b == 5)
{
    printf( " This is the correct statement")
}
else
    printf(" This is the wrong statement")
}
```

Output:

This is the wrong statement

In the above program, the second statement is displayed as a result because one of the two statements is not true.

b) OR operator

This is a logical operator that displays the result even if any one of them is true. If both statements are not true then the other statement will be executed as a result.

```
#include<math.h>
//This is used to import mathematical functions
main()
{
    int a=3;
    int b=6;
    int c= a*b;
    if( a == 3 OR b == 5)
    {
        printf( " This is the correct statement")
```

```
    }
    else
        printf(" This is the wrong statement")
}
```

Output:

This is the correct statement

c) NOT operator

NOT operator is used to display when a statement is false. If not the other statement will be executed.

```
#include<math.h>
//This is used to import mathematical functions
main()
{
    int first=3;
    if( first == 3 NOT b == 5)
        printf(" This is the wrong statement")
}
```

Output:

This is the wrong statement

Conditional and Loop operations

a) Conditional

Conditional statements are used in the C programming language to make decisions. They are advanced components of C and can be used in nested structures too. They consist of an if and an else statement.

Here is the format:

if(condition)

{

   // Enter the statement

}

else

   // Enter the statement

Here is an example:

a=7;

if(a==3)

printf(" This is true")

else

printf("This is false)

Output:

This is false

b) Loop statements

Loop statements are used in C programming to do repetitive tasks. Here, we will use for loop to help you understand the impact of the looping operations.

Here is the format:

```
for(i=value;i++;variable)
{
   // Enter the statements
}
```

Here is an example:

```
int a=0;
for(i=0;i>10;i++)
{
   i =10;
   i++;
   printf(" The results: %d',a)
}
```

With this, we have completed a comprehensive chapter that explains to you about various operations that are available in the C.

In the next chapter, we will in detail discuss structures one of the most important components of C programming language.

Follow along!

Chapter 8: Structures

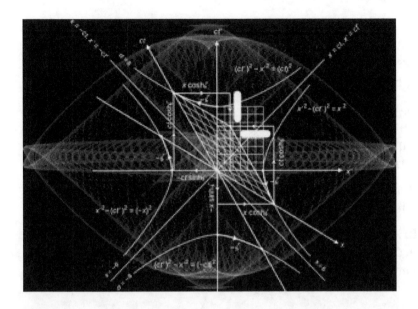

In programming languages, we often use interlinked variables to solve problems. C programming language provides structures as a basis to categorize interlinked entities while programming.

In object orient paradigm supported languages, classes are used to create a linkage between the variables. However, C is a procedural language that doesn't support classes.

With continuous development, C has found a way to counter this advantage of object-oriented programming languages using structures.

Structures do the same work as classes do but more effectively.

We will also provide various examples to help you understand the importance of structures.

Follow along!

Why is grouping necessary?

Usually, programming languages are with a large number of system functions. You can also create a lot of global and local variables during the creation of software.

When the programming complexity increases it makes things difficult to organize and maintain. So, to categorize variables and functions the concept of structures is introduced in the C programming language.

It serves an important purpose and can make programming effective.

In the next section, we will explain about the programmatical interpretation of structures in larger detail. Let us go!

What are the structures?

During the initial stages of C language development variables are first used to store values and functions to apply features on those values. However, with the increase in the data arrays are invented to store multiple values with a single entity name.

Arrays can be one-dimensional and two-dimensional and can store a lot of elements. The demerit of arrays is that all available elements in the arrays can be only of a single data type.

To counter this demerit in arrays, structures are developed. To make you understand in layman terms, structures are discrete programming components that can store variables of different data types. For example, you can create an int variable and a float variable at the same time using a structure.

To help you delve into the theoretical understanding of structures let us consider an example. Imagine a bookstore that requires a program to handle the book operations.

Here are some of the data types that can be used:

Bookname of string type

BookId of Integer type

Price of Integer type

Author name of string type

Using structures, you can create all these variables at once and can use them in multiple instances. All the variables that are created while a structure is represented as members of the structures.

You can define whether or not to use these members in the other parts of the programming code. There is a lot of customization in structures making it one of the most important components of C programming language.

To make things more interesting you can also use arrays and pointers during the structure creation.

You can also create a nested structure to further increase the effectiveness of the program.

In the next sections of this chapter, we will discuss all of these details about structures in detail.

Let us go!

How to define a structure?

The structure is a programming entity that holds different types of variables as explained before. C programing language uses certain varied distinctions to declare a structure.

Here is the format:

struct {Enter the name of the structure here}

While creating a structure, all you need to do is enter the 'struct' keyword along with the name you want to give it. After that, you need to create a body of the structure with defined variables using the format given below.

```
struct sample
{
    int number;
    char sex;
    int houseno;
    string name;
};
```

In the above program, the declared variables are called the members of the structure.

They can be used with access modifiers to make them global variables or not.

Always remember that you need to use a semicolon to end a structure.

If not, you will be shown a syntax error.

How to use structure variables in the main function?

Now, we need to know the way to use structure members in the main function. Whenever a structure is defined, they should be allowed to be used by another entity.

Here is the format:

main()

{

struct sample entity1,entity2;

}

Now, when the struct variables are declared both of them(i.e entity1 and entity2) can have each instance of the member that is present with the structure.

How to access these structure entities?

All you need to do is use the dot '.' symbol to make the declared variables in the main function access the members of the structure.

Here is the format:

entity1.name;

Use the above format to print out the elements present in a structure.

With this, we have discussed structures in brief. To learn about structures in much more depth we recommend you to look at the official documentation. In the next chapter, we will discuss in-depth the manipulation of strings. Follow along!

Chapter 9: Manipulation

Strings are one of the most important and effective datatypes of the C programming language.

A lot of program user interfaces use strings to get implemented.

Strings can be used to store a lot of data. A lot of machine learning and system applications import data in the form of strings. Manipulations are a technique to control the strings data that we have access to. Strings can be manipulated to get reversed or divided according to our instructions. C language provides a library to implement the procedures of string manipulation.

In this chapter, we will discuss various system functions that can change the course of strings. Look at the examples we have provided in this chapter carefully and try to implement those system functions in your programs.

Let us go!

Why is Manipulation necessary?

Manipulation of strings is necessary because changing the strings manually is burdensome and time-consuming. Using the library functions, we can change an array of strings within no time

. Also, C programming language provides tens of system functions to manipulate strings which are often complex and difficult for the programmers to handle.

For example, A string can be reversed automatically using the reverse () function.

How Manipulations can be implemented?

First of all, to implement manipulations on the string data we possess we need to import the string library that holds a lot of manipulative functions.

Here is the format:

#include <string.h>

After importing the library, you can call the functions to the string variable or array present to look at the results. You can look at the C documentation to know about various string manipulative functions.

In this chapter, we will look at some of the most important string manipulative functions with examples.

Follow along!

Manipulative string functions

a) Concatenating two strings

Using this manipulative function, you can combine two strings that are present. We will provide an example to help you understand this function in detail.

Here is the program code:

```
// You need to import the string manipulation function library
#include<string.h>
main()
{
// Enter the first string
stringsample1 = " This is great";
// Enter the second string
stringsample2 = " This is awful"
// Now you need to enter the string concatenation function
string result = *strcat (stringsample1,stringsample2)
// Now print the result
printf(" Here is the result : result", %s)
}
```

Output:

Here is the result:

ThisisgreatThisisawful

You can find out from the result that the two strings have been concatenated.

b)Comparing two strings

This is a manipulative function where two strings are compared. The results will be in integer format where the negative number represents that the first string has more similarities than the second and the positive integer represent the latter. If 0 is displayed then it informs that the two strings are equal. We will give an example to help you understand this manipulative function in detail.

Here is the program code:

// You need to import the string manipulation function library

#include<string.h>

main()

{

// Enter the first string

stringsample1 = " Hello America";

// Enter the second string

stringsample2 = " Hello Newyork"

// Now you need to enter the string compare function

string result = *strcmp (stringsample1,stringsample2)

// Now print the result

printf(" Here is the result : result", %s)

}

Output:

Here is the result:

8

By the result, we understand that the string 2 differs from string 1 with 8 characters.

c) Copy strings

This manipulative function will help you to copy one string to another string. This is usually used in the advanced implementation of office programs.

Here is the program code:

```
// You need to import the string manipulation function library
#include<string.h>
main()
{
// Enter the first string
stringsample1 = " ";
// Enter the second string
stringsample2 = " This is copied"
// Now you need to enter the string copy function
string result = *strcpy (stringsample1,stringsample2)
// Now print the result
printf(" Here is the result : result", %s)
}
```

Output:

Here is the result:

This is copied

d) To upper case

With this string function, all the characters will be changed to upper case letters. Look at an example to understand it in a much better way.

Here is the program code:

```
// You need to import the string manipulation function library

#include<string.h>

main()

{

// Enter the first string

stringsample1 = " This is not easy";

// Now you need to enter the string upper case function

string result = struprcase(stringsample1)

// Now print the result

printf(" Here is the result : result", %s)

}
```

Output:

Here is the result:

THIS IS NOT EASY

e) To find the string length

With this, we can find the number of characters in the string. The string length will be displayed in the number format as a result.

Look at the below example to understand it in a better way.

Here is the program code:

```
// You need to import the string manipulation function library

#include<string.h>

main()

{
```

```
// Enter the first string
stringsample1 = " Hello America";
// Now you need to enter the string length function
string result = strlen(stringsample1)
// Now print the result
printf(" Here is the result : result", %s)
}
```

Output:

Here is the result:

11

f) To lowercase

This is a string manipulative function that can be used to display all the characters to lower case letters.

Here is the program code:

```
// You need to import the string manipulation function library
#include<string.h>
main()
{
// Enter the first string
stringsample1 = "This is great!";
// Now you need to enter the string lowercase function
string result = strlwr (stringsample1)
// Now print the result
printf(" Here is the result : result", %s)
}
```

Output:

Here is the result:

this is great

g) String error

The string error function is used to display error for a particular problem. This can be implemented easily as shown below.

Here is the program code:

```
// You need to import the string manipulation function library

#include<string.h>

main()

{

// Enter the first string

stringsample1 = " Hello America";

// Now you need to enter the string error function

string result = strerr (stringsample/0," You can't divide a string with 0")

// Now print the result

printf(" Here is the result : result", %s)

}
```

Output:

Here is the result:

You can't divide a string with 0

With this, we have completed a brief introduction to string manipulations in C programming language. In the next chapter, we will discuss constants in detail. Follow along!

Chapter 10: Constants

In programming languages, variables are used to store literal values. These literal values are usually called as constants in mathematical terms. Constants are important to give a certain value to the variable that you have created. Constant values can be easily replaced or manipulated with the help of functions.

Constants are also divided into different categories depending on the storage value. In this chapter, we will give a thorough explanation of constants with a lot of examples. Follow along to know more about it.

What are constants?

According to layman terms constant is a value that is fixed and holds a literal value in the canonical terms. Almost all programming languages deal with constants.

In a programmatical sense, they are called literals because they cannot be replaced unless a variable is changed.

In the next chapters of this book, we will discuss various data types that are declared when a variable is initiated or created.

For now, remember that data types are used to define constant values. The sole difference between literals and identifiers is that they cannot be changed.

Some of the famous constant values are integer constants, floating-point constants, and enumeration constants.

In the next section, we will comprehensively discuss them. Follow along!

Integer constants

An integer is a common way to define numbers in the programming languages.

In normal mathematics scenarios, there are usually different types of mathematical systems to denote numbers. For example, the decimal system is a mathematical number system. In the same way, programming languages can also determine various number systems and constants.

Integer constants can be normally represented in three systems in C programming language namely decimal, octal and hexadecimal.

Here are the examples:

3778

// This is a decimal number system

/* They usually represent numbers from 0 to 9 */

4664

// This is an octal representation

/* They only represent numbers from 0 to 7 */

0xdef

// This is a hexadecimal representation

Integer constants can be used in arithmetic and mathematical calculations. They can also be used in performing logical evaluations. A lot of hexadecimal notation is usually used to represent computer memory locations.

Floating-point constants

As explained before, integer constants cannot hold all the different types of mathematical representations that are available.

They are only created for storing simple numerical literals. Floating-point constants are much more advanced entities that can hold different mathematical constants such as exponential and negative.

Here are some of the examples:

3.24343

// This is a floating-point constant

3.894e

// This is an exponential constant

-445.3545

// This is a negative floating-point literal

Floating-point literals can be easily used to manipulate complex computer programs.

They can also be used to perform logical evaluations and operations.

Character literals

Characters are usually single letter arguments. They can be used for the smart processing of data in the program. However, C programming language has implemented character literals to create new lines and new tabs.

/n,/x are some of the examples of the character literals. Here is a good description of them.

1) /n

This is a character literal that can be used to create a new line in the program result.

2) /t

This is a character literal that can be used to create a new tab in the program result

Character literals are often used to determine newly created functions. They can also be used in the place of function arguments.

String literals

String literals are usual string data type entities that can hold a lot of continuous data. A lot of computer programs use string literals to input data.

Here is an example:

" This is a new world. This is the end of the world too"

// This is a string literal

How to define a constant?

Apart from using normal equivalent literals, you can also create constant literals that can be used at any part of the program just by calling the name of the constant.

Here is the format:

#define {Enter the identifier and constant value here}

For example:

#define Area=25metere

In the program, whenever Area is called in a function or using a template the constant will be sued.

There is also another way:

You can also use the constant keyword and the data type to give a literal value to the variable. This is used in a lot of system application libraries to start things in a better way.

const {Enter the data type} {Enter the value}

For example:

const int stupid = 64;

You can use the following constant and print results whenever needed using the %d notation.

These are some of the famous ways to define and create constants. In the next section, we will describe different types of constants based on storage values.

Specifiers

Constants in C programming language usually have specifiers to enhance the performance of the program. These specifiers will help you regulate the storage memory allocation.

For example, you can use long along with int data type to deal with larger values.

You can also use small with float literals to deal with less negative values.

Why specifiers are important?

Sometimes when we are dealing with programming code you can't understand how to allocate resources so that the programs will effectively.

For example, a buffer overflow execution error with constant literal values can make things difficult for the processor. So, when you are dealing with larger values it makes sense to predefine them to allocate sufficient resources for them.

In the same manner, mentioning specifiers can help the computer to understand that fewer resources are sufficient for the program. Specifiers increase program interactivity between the system allocations and resources.

Here are some of the examples:

long int first = 372737LL

small int second = 3

With this, we have completed a brief explanation about constants and literal values.

This is a comprehensive topic and we suggest you experiment with some of the code provided here on your compilers.

In the next chapter, we will start discussing Arrays in detail. Follow along!

Chapter 11: Arrays

Usually, in the programming languages, variables are used to store values. They are designated with the help of data types and can be used across functions, structures, and every other programming component.

Despite all the advantages variables possess they are quite useless when dealing with large data.

For dealing with larger data programming languages use structures called Arrays.

In this chapter, we will in detail discuss the importance of arrays along with its implementations and examples.

Follow along!

Why are Arrays necessary?

Arrays are a set of items that are ordered in a sequence. All the items can be easily pulled out whenever necessary by the program.

The usage of Arrays became familiar when programmers started to develop complex and large applications that deal with huge data. At the initial stages of computing, there was only a necessity of a few inputs and calculations. However, with the expansion and popularization of programming languages, people started to input large numbers of data.

For a few years, people used variables to do bulk operations. However, as data increased, they understood how difficult it is to organize and compare multi-data using variables.

To counter this problem Arrays are first introduced in the C language and since then Arrays are an essential component and a necessity to develop complex and large applications.

How to define an array?

Just like every other programming component arrays are required to define using a predefined format.

Arrays consist of index and subscript to easily maintain the set of values.

Here is the format for an array:

Arrayname = subscript[]

// This is the array designation

x[]

// This is the subscript of the file

[1]

// This is called index in terms of programming

For example:

example = sample[5]

Here 'example' is the array name and has a 5 set of values. Here the values are represented using the subscript.

For your better understanding, here are the set of variables that are enclosed in this array:

sample[0]

sample[1]

sample[2]

sample[3]

sample[4]

Here 0,1,2,3,4 are called the index of the array.

Note: Remember that the index of the array starts from 0 but not from 1.

A lot of people confuse with this simple mathematical notation while dealing with operations.

Advantages of Arrays

As explained before, arrays are extensively used to deal with high-level efficient programs. You can use them to determine or change the features of system-level software. Arrays are also easy to identify and can save a lot of programming resources.

Apart from being an efficient programming component arrays can be used in a lot of looping programs that deal with repetitive tasks.

Note:

In the subscript of the array bracket, you can also use mathematical expressions and statements.

For example, array = dude[integer/2]

How arrays manage memory?

Arrays use the stack principle to store data in the memory locations. If you want to add or delete an element from the arrays you can only do it at the end of an array.

Arrays are stored cumulatively and sequentially in the storage points.

For example, if the first element of the array is stored in 111a of the computer memory. Then the next four elements will be stored in the memory locations 111b,111c,111d. When an array is created memory allocation is done at the beginning.

How to use arrays as counters?

Counter statements and operators are used to increase the data or variable literals exponentially. For example, you can multiply 100 times of a number using the counter statements. Arrays can also be used as counters in the C programming language.

We will use an example to help you understand the C language usage of arrays:

```
#include {enter the library here]
void ()
{
  int samplearray[10];
  for ( i=0; i++; samplearray)
  {
    scanf (" %n, " Use this")
    printf( " Enter the values")
    samplearray++;
  }
}
```

Here in this program, the counter values are automatically increased by using the output statements.

This program also uses Scanf to recognize the array index values. Look at the samplearray[] to understand arrays.

The index is automatically using the loop statements that are provided. Arrays used in this program make sus understand that arrays are variables that can store data with high precision.

In the next sections, we will learn about the initialization of variables and the multidimensional array's importance in detail.

Follow along!

Initializing arrays

Arrays are used as an easy way to store multiple values. All these values can be updated manually or automatically using default programs. Arrays can be initialized individually using the following format.

datatype arrayname[subscript] = {}

In the braces, you can enter the values of the arrays. The array subscript is counted with the order of the arrays inside the braces.

Here is an example:

int sample[5] = {3,4,5,,7,8}

Now, the arrays are initialized and hold a certain value. For example, sample[4] has a value of 8. This is an easy way to initialize variables. You can also use loop statements to automatically fill arrays while they were being used for functions.

Arrays can be initialized for any data type.

Characters and float data types are extensively used while initializing arrays.

All you need to change the data type value in the initialization format.

Another way to initialize:

You can use for loops to initialize arrays. It is often considered difficult to i individually enter the values for the array elements. So, if you already have data in a text file then you can use array system functions to scan and input the values in the array.

Here is the program:

```
for(i=0;i++;array)
{
  array[i];
  i+=;
  array[0] = array[0]+=1;
}
```

With this format, you can enter values easily into arrays. You can also initialize char arrays using the above format.

Constants with Arrays

You can use const identifiers to deal with variables that cannot change the array specifications. A lot of elements in the array remain empty and will not serve any purpose for the system resources.

Here is the code:

```
const array[] = {}
```

Multidimensional arrays

Multidimensional arrays are special programming components that can be used to create advanced data structures and matrix operations.

Here is the format:

```
arrayname[][]
```

The first value is called the row of the array and the second value is known as the column of the array.

When we multiply both values, we get the total number of elements present in the array.

Here is the code:

array[2][3]

Here, the number of elements is 6.

With this, we have completed a brief explanation about arrays.

In the next chapter, we will discuss time functions in detail. Follow along!

Chapter 12: Time Functions

C programming language provides various standard libraries that perform different actions. We have already discussed input, output and string manipulative functions. C programming also provides various standard mathematic functions.

In this chapter, we will discuss time and date functions that are quite essential for programmers. Time and date functions will be handy while creating programs that need automatic functioning according to the date and time.

For example, an alarm app needs to access standard time and date functions.

Try to look out at the examples and use them according to your convenience.

Follow along!

How to declare time functions?

As we are aware of the previous chapters, to import time and date functions we need to enter the preprocessing library at the starting of the code. Here, the library name is time.h.

Here is the format:

#include<time.h>

All the functions that are present in the time standard library use two types of format to represent time. In the first standard, time is the default in every region.

The time and date will be according to the Georgian calendar.

This format is automatically used by the C standard library whenever a library function is instantiated.

The second format is much more complex and deals with local time. It differs from region to region according to the location you are in.

This local time is also said to use day times saving functionality to give accurate results.

In the next section, we will in detail discuss the most important time manipulative functions with examples. Follow along!

Time and Date functions

a) Clock function

This is a standard time function that describes the time that the processor uses. The processing time is calculated right from the program that has been instantiated.

Here is the program:

```
#include <time.h>

// This is the standard time library that needs to be imported

main()
{
// Create a variable to store the result

float example;

result = clock_t (example);

// This is the clock function that prints out the processing time

printf( " Here is the result: %f', result)

// We print out the result of the time function
}
```

Output:

Here is the result:

4.34224 s

The output that has been displayed is the processing time for this particular program.

b) difftime

This is a complex manipulative function that can be used to find the difference between the two calendar times provided.

Here is the program:

```
#include <time.h>
```

// This is the standard time library that needs to be imported

```
main()
{
```

// Create a variable to store the result

```
float difference;
```

```
result = difftime (difference1,difference2);
```

// This is used to find the difference between two calendar times

```
printf( " Here is the result: %f', result)
```

// We print out the result of the time function

```
}
```

Output:

Here is the result:

12h32m32s

c) time function

By using this function, you can display the exact time at this moment. You can change the format of the time displayed using the spacebar option.

Here is the program:

```
#include <time.h>

// This is the standard time library that needs to be imported

main()
{
// Create a variable to store the result
float exacttime;
result = time(exacttime);
// This is used to display the exact time at present
printf( " Here is the result: %f', result)
// We print out the result of the time function
}
```

Output:

Here is the result:

12:23:21

d) asctime

The asctime is used to display the time in a different display format that is compatible with ASCII format.

Here is the program:

```
#include <time.h>
```

// This is the standard time library that needs to be imported

```
main()
{
```

// Create a variable to store the result

```
float format;
```

```
result = asci (format);
```

// This is used to display time in ASCII format

```
printf( " Here is the result: %f', result)
```

// We print out the result of the time function

```
}
```

Output:

Here is the result:

Sat Oct 22 03:11:34 2020

e) ctime

This will change the local time of your region to the default Georgian calendar that is used by the programming environment.

Here is the program:

```
#include <time.h>
```

// This is the standard time library that needs to be imported

```
main()
{
```

// Create a variable to store the result

```
float change;

result = ctime (change);
```

// This is the default georgian calendar time

```
printf( " Here is the result: %f', result)
```

// We print out the result of the time function

```
}
```

Output:

Here is the result:

22:12:23 changed

f) Local time

This will display according to the local time of your location. For example, PST time.

Here is the program:

#include <time.h>

// This is the standard time library that needs to be imported

main()

{

// Create a variable to store the result

float time;

result = local (time);

// This is used to display the local time

printf(" Here is the result: %f', result)

// We print out the result of the time function

}

Output:

Here is the result:

12:12:32

g) gmtime

This is used to display the default UTC according to the ISO conventions.

Here is the program:

```
#include <time.h>
```

// This is the standard time library that needs to be imported

```
main()
{
```

// Create a variable to store the result

```
float default;
```

```
result = gm (default);
```

// This is the clock function that displays UTC time

```
printf( " Here is the result: %f', result)
```

// We print out the result of the time function

```
}
```

Output:

Here is the result:

12:32:45

h) mktime

This format will display the week and month of the calendar in a good format.

Here is the program:

```
#include <time.h>
// This is the standard time library that needs to be imported
main()
{
// Create a variable to store the result
float calendar;
result = mktime (calendar);
// This prints out the calendar in a good format
printf( " Here is the result: %f', result)
// We print out the result of the time function
}
```

Output:

Here is the result:

JULY 12 2020 THURSDAY 22Hours:32Minutes: 23Second:32Milliseconds

With this, we have completed a comprehensive chapter that describes various time functions that are available in C programming language.

In the next chapter, we will discuss in detail about variables in depth.

Let us go!

Chapter 13: Variables

Variables are one of the important components of any programming language.

They store values and are often used in functions, structures, and templates. It is always recommended to learn about variables in depth before starting to create complex programs. I

n this chapter, we will discuss variables with various examples.

Follow along!

What are the variables?

It is important to understand the historical significance of memory management before understanding variables. Before the invention of programming languages, all the memory is managed using the binary sequences.

Everything is needed to be done in the hardcoded away. All of the significant memory locations are stored using a specific memory address in the computer.

However, with time these hardcoded methods are proven to be ineffective.

A lot of high-level programming languages started to use variables which are a symbolic representation of the memory locations.

How are the variables assigned?

First of all, remember that to create variables you need to define data types. These are also used for assigning literal constants. Data types are an easy way to distinguish the variables.

Why are data types necessary?

Imagine that you need to create a program that takes only characters as input values. It is not feasible to use strings that take up storage memory. Data types are used for faster memory processing and effective storage management. There are different types of data types such as integers, floating-point numbers and double. Data types can also be used to store pointers that store the variable address. We will learn about pointers in-depth in the upcoming chapters.

Rules for creating variables

Variables are defined using certain preconceived instructions. They are often started using an underscore. However, remember that variables are not case sensitive. so, both upper case and lower-case letters can be used to create variables.

Note: Reserved keywords cannot be used as the name of variables. There are more than 60 default reserved keywords in the C programming language that cannot be used as identifiers.

You can find out the reserved keyword list from the official website.

Tip:

Make variable names simple. It is not feasible to use complex long names to declare variables. You can, of course, do it but it is not a good programming practice.

Here are some of the good variable declaration examples:

ramdas

_Usa

Randis

Here are some of the bad variable declaration examples:

1sery

thisisalongvariablename

*gdhd

pointer

In the next section, we will in detail discuss data types that are essential for the variables.

a) Numbers

Numbers are the most important data entity that is used in programming. All the mathematical equations and algorithms require integral constants to solve the specific problem. C

programming uses various data types to declare numerical variables.

i) int

This is the most common data variable that is used to declare numerical variables. int cannot store decimal values and is said to occupy till ten digits. It stores a few bytes of data whenever a variable is declared. While implementing the printing statements, %n can be used to print the variables with the int data type.

You can also use %x and %o to print the stored values in different formats such as octal and hexadecimal. Usually, int data type occupies 32 bytes of storage in the memory.

ii) float

Floating-point numbers are used to represent decimal and scientific notations. It can occupy up to 64 digits and can be used while developing complex scientific applications. A lot of exponential problems and modulus calculations can be done with the help of floating-point literal.

When printing the output statements %f is used as a notation.

iii) double

Double is the advanced expansion of floating-point literals. In double both negative and positive decimal notations can be used. They can extend up to 128 digits. You can use %f or % e to print the double literals as an output.

b) Characters

After numbers, the most important data types should be of characters and strings. Almost all applications rely on characters to communicate with the users. Here are the character datatypes that C programming language offers.

i) character

Characters are single literal expressions that can be used in a program. They are usually used to input responses from the user while running the program. Characters occupy very less memory storage and are considered good for the allocation of program resources.

%c is usually used to designate the output of characters in the programming languages.

ii) Strings

Strings are the advanced implementation of character expressions. In the real world, it is not feasible to just use characters for expressing entities. Strings are one of the often-used data types while developing computer programs.

%s is usually used to designate strings in the programming languages.

c) Boolean data types

Programming is a logical process where the computer should often decide between the choices that are given to it. Sometimes they may be random but they are usually followed by a logical equivalence. All the conditional and loop statements depend on Boolean data types.

Usually, there are only two Boolean data types that are true and false.

There are defined by the identifier _Bool. Bool variables can change the understanding of the program execution process.

Here is an example:

if (x >3)

{

  _Bool = true;

   printf(" Enter the condition here")

}

In the above example of a C program, the program is executed only when the logical statement is true. If it doesn't satisfy the logical statement then the program will end and give compilation errors.

Boolean data types are essential for a lot of logical programs and software.

With this, we have completed a brief explanation about variables and data types.

Variable declaration and assignment can be thoroughly understood only when you practice coding a lot of programs.

 We recommend you to look at different open source projects to understand the importance of variables. In the next chapter, we will learn about pointers in depth.

Follow along!

Chapter 14: Pointers

This chapter is a clear introduction to one of the most controversial and most discussed features of C language that is pointers. No other programming languages provide pointers as a feature in their index.

The extremely low-level interaction with the hardware resources is one of the reasons why pointers have become a reality in the C programming language.

In this chapter, we will give a short introduction to pointers with several examples.

Follow along to know more about it.

What are the pointers?

First of all, to understand the concept of pointers we need to let you understand the process of indirection in computing and in real life. Let us imagine that you are the manager of a book store.

A customer approaches you and asks for a book that is not available in the book store. So, what will you do next? You will inform the wholesale book supplier to get the book for your customer.

That wholesale supplier you contacted will reach out to other book suppliers to give it to you.

So, if you look at this example carefully you 'the manager' just acted as a medium to deliver the book for your customer. You did not directly go to the book supplier to get that desired book.

This process of mediating things to complete a task is known as indirection. Pointers in C follows the same mechanism. They provide access to the data value you are searching for.

Just like how indirection reduces cost fares for the manager of the book store, pointers help programmers to strategically manage resources.

In the next section, we will in detail discuss declaring a pointer with examples. Follow along!

How to declare pointers?

First of all, you need to create a variable that can be used to declare pointer variables.

Here is the variable:

int sample = 34;

As soon as you declare a variable it is declared a storage location in the system. You can check it using the ampersand symbol '&'.

For example:

&sample;

Output:

0dfd656

The memory location will always be in a hexadecimal format.

In the next section, you need to declare a variable that can act as a pointer.

All you need to do is add an asterisk in front of the identifier name to declare it as a pointer.

Here is the format:

int *data_pointer

The above statement roughly states that a pointer of an integer data type with the name data_pointer is created. After the pointer is declared you can use it to point out to other variables.

In the next step, we will use this pointer to store the first variable location that we have created. This will make you understand the importance of pointers in memory allocation statements.

Here is the format:

data_pointer = &sample

Now, whenever you call the pointer, you will get the output as the storage location of the sample variable.

Output:

0dfd656

You can also use an asterisk as an indirection operator to denote all the variables that a pointer holds.

Here is the format:

*data_pointer

Output:

sample

With this, we have completed a brief explanation about the declaration about the pointers.

In the next section, we will in detail discuss some of the advantages that pointers possess in the C programming language.

Follow along!

Advantages of pointers

1) With the help of pointers, you can create a more optimized code. For example, if you use static buffers to enclose a large list of values instead of pointers, they may lead to buffer flow errors. However, with the usage of pointers, memory allocation works perfectly and makes you create more complex programs.

2) Pointers are an essential component that needs to be used while dealing with multidimensional arrays that hold a lot of elements. Pointers are also extensively used to create data structures such as heaps, graphs, and trees.

3) Dynamic memory allocation is very essential if you have fewer computing resources. Pointers are the only way to maintain an equilibrium between the resources available. If not of pointers, C programming language will become clumsy and may need to deal with a lot of run-time errors before starting the execution of the program.

4) They are very useful when you are trying to do repetitive tasks such as refreshing an element or for sorting algorithms.

Null pointers

Null pointers are a special type of pointers where they are pointed out to a null value. Null pointers are used when they are not allowed to produce any return values.

Here is an example:

int *pointer = NULL;

Now, whenever you call the pointer in a function you will get a null value as a result.

How to use pointers in Functions?

Pointers and functions can be used cumulatively to produce results. Pointers can use functions as return statements and values. Whereas, functions can also use points as their function parameters and arguments.

Here is how you can use a pointer as a function argument:

functionname(data_pointer)

When the logical equivalence statements are written they take the data_pointer argument as a pointer.

You can use this argument in the function body as:

void main()
{
  functionname int *data_point;
}

When the pointer is called it displays the storage location as the output result.

Remember that by changing the function arguments using a pointer you can change the instances of the pointer but you cannot change the actual storage location of the variable that you are dealing with.

Pointers along with functions can be used for faster results in software.

Using this method, you can easily exchange values between two variables.

Here is the program:

```
main()
{
    variable1 = data_pointer
    varaible2 = *data_pointer
    result = &variable2
    varaiabe2 = *varaible1
}
```

When the results are produced you will find out that the values of the variables have been exchanged.

How to use pointers for arrays?

Arrays can also use pointers to deal with complex multi-dimensional operations. They are used in both one-dimensional and two-dimensional arrays.

Here is a program:

```
main()
{
  int variable[] = data_pointer
   &varaible[] = *data_pointer
   *data_pointer = int variable[]
}
```

In the above program, pointers are pointed out to arrays. They are very useful if you are dealing with a huge chunk of data.

With this, we have completed a brief introduction to pointers.

In the next chapter, we will with examples give a brief description of double pointers.

Follow along to know more about it in detail.

Chapter 15: Dual pointers

In the previous chapter, we have discussed pointers in detail. We have given you various examples to help you understand the impact of pointers in C programming.

This chapter introduces a double pointer (also called as Pointer to Pointer) in short with few examples.

Follow along to understand about double pointers.

Let us go!

What is a double pointer?

As discussed in the previous chapter pointers usually point out to the variable location they are assigned to and they are represented by an asterisk (*). Double pointers are a little bit advanced way to store address values.

When a double pointer is created it is designed in a way such that it can store the location value of the first pointer that is been assigned with storage value.

The double-pointer is represented with a double asterisk (**). You can further continue this concept with three, four and an infinite pointer to pointer sequences.

Declaring a double-pointer

Declaring double pointers are quite similar to the declaration of pointers.

All you need to do is add an extra asterisk alongside it. This is similar if you are implementing it in arrays or in structures.

Here is the format:

string **ptr;

// A double pointer is created

Understanding Double pointers

In this section, we will help you understand double pointers in-depth with the help of an example below.

Here is the program code:

```
#include {Enter the libraries here}
// This is an example for double pointer
int main()
{
    string value = "Gold";
  // Now we will create a pointer
    int *create;
 // Now we will create a double-pointer
    int **double;
 // Now will display the storage value
    create = &value;
  // Now will display the storage of pointer
    double = &create;
  // We will just print out the result
    printf("Value of the variable = %d\n", var );
    printf(" Let us display pointer entity = %f\n", *create );
    printf(" Let us display double pointer = %f\n", **double);
  }
```

Output:

Value of variable = GOLD

Pointer entity: 2s737

Double pointer entity: 0x776

When you look at the programming code, you will understand how double pointers are created.

In the next chapter, we will learn about creating a C program using an IDE.

Follow along!

Chapter 16: Creating a C program

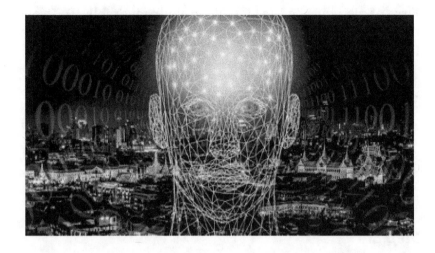

In the previous chapters of this book, you have learned about various components that make up an effective program.

This chapter is a brief one that explains you a step by step instruction to create a C program in an integrated development environment.

This short chapter will let you understand the basic process of the C programming procedure.

How to create a C program?

Step 1:

First of all, you need to download your favorable IDE from the official website. In this chapter, we will use the NetBeans IDE to run the C program that we are going to create.

Step 2:

After installing the NetBeans IDE open it from the menu and create a new C file from the create menu in the bottom tray of the system. Make sure the extension of the file is .C. If not, the program will not get compiled by the IDE

Step 3:

Now, enter the given program in the IDE

```
// Program to check whether a number is even or odd
#include<stdio.h>
// This is called a pre processing library
void main()
{
    int  sample = 6;
    if( sample /2 )
    printf(" This is an even number');
    else
    print(" This is an odd number');
}
```

Step 4:

After entering the following C program in the IDE save it from the options on the menu. After saving it you are now already to compile it in the NetBeans IDE. Use the compile button from the menu. You can use F3 to compile.

Step 5:

The compilation procedure will start and will show success if there are no errors. However, if there are any errors in the program they will be shown up in sequential order.

Step 6:

After compiling and if there are no errors you can click the Run (F5) button to display the output. You can also debug the code while it is running.

This is the normal procedure to create, compile and run a C program in an IDE.

In the next chapter, we will discuss dealing with errors in detail.

Let us go!

Chapter 17: Common errors in C programming

In the previous chapters of this book, we have discussed various components and lexical syntax that can help us create an effective programming code.

That particular effective program is then compiled to run in any operating system. However, the compiler will check the whole programming code and decide whether it is good by itself to run or not.

If there are any errors related to syntax, function or run-time the program will terminate immediately and show the reasons for the error.

As a programmer, it is an essential skill to have sufficient information about the types of errors you are going to deal with.

If you can't understand the complexity of error you have encountered then it is very difficult to create effective code. So, to make you aware of the essential information of the types of errors available in C language we provided this chapter.

Learn carefully and try to use google if you ever face any error.

Clearing errors is the best way to learn to program.

Let us go!

What is an error?

Usually, programs expect a certain numerical, analytical or logical result to the program they have compiled. If you are unable to get the desired result for your program then it is called an error. Remember that a bug is not an error.

A bug is a programmatical mistake that will let exploiters take advantage of it. Usually, bad programming principles cause an error.

Errors are made by programmers because of a mistake in syntax or because of not following basic programming rules of that particular language.

For example, you can't use reserved keywords as a variable in C programming language, So, if you use 'for' keyword in a variable then it will show you a syntax error. [for is a reserved keyword]

Errors in C

C programming language is famously known for its unique way of representing error syntaxes in the output results. Unlike other high-level programming languages, C is said to be strict with case sensitive letters and whitespaces.

It is naturally a difficult language to learn because it strictly follows all the guidelines.

In this section, we will in detail explain the different errors that are available in C programming language.

Follow along!

a) Syntax error

The syntax is like grammar to a programming language. Without exact precise statements, the compiler will not allow you to proceed further.

In layman terms, syntax errors appear in C language when there is a mistake related to the syntax of the program. For example, wrong variable names and data types can cause syntax errors.

Different programming languages use different syntax rules. So, if you are new to any programming language, we suggest you learn in-depth about different syntactical rules that the language uses. It is often easy to debug syntax errors because the compiler shows the exact code line for you.

All you need to do is use the correct syntax in the place of incorrect syntax to make the program work.

Here is an example:

int a= 5.7493;

Output:

Syntax error. You can't proceed further

The above example ended up with a syntax error because the variable is declared as an int data type value but is given a floating-point literal.

b) Runtime errors

Runtime errors appear when a programmer does a mistake in the program operations that needs to be committed. In simple terms, runtime errors appear when the errors are related to the technical analysis of the program.

For example, if you call a function that is not yet created it gives a run time error. Run time errors are a little bit difficult to clear off because of the ambiguity they possess.

Some of the example of run time errors:

1) Making bad and undefined calculations is a classic use case. For example, dividing a number by zero is a good way to understand it. When you divide any number by zero it is of undefined format. A computer doesn't know how to represent or output the result that doesn't exist. So, it displays runtime errors during the compilation process.

2) A lot of file management operations often end up with run time errors. For example, opening a file that is not yet even created is not possible. So, an ambiguity is created and a run time error will be displayed.

3) A lot of complex programs also face run time errors when all the memory is allocated to the program. For example, buffer overflows can cause a run time error.

Here is an example:

int a=3;

a/0;

Output:

Runtime error -- You cannot divide a variable with zero

c)Logical error

Programming is a lexical language that uses different identifiers and literals to complete tasks with a computer. Programming logics are incomplete without logical statements and expressions. For example, OR AND NOT all are considered as logical operators that can be used to compare expressions and statements.

Logical equivalence statements are also often prone to errors due to the ambiguity they create in the programming languages.

Logical errors are often difficult to notice because they will not completely stop the compilation process but will give faulty results. They are like machine learning applications to say in layman terms.

Here is an example:

int a=+b;

Here an unnecessary assignment operator is used resulting in faulty execution of the program.

Warnings in C programming

Warnings are different from errors in the programming language. Warnings will not stop the execution of the program. They act as signals that inform you about the ineffectiveness of the program.

Compilers suspect that the code you have written is not good in terms of execution. So, when you detect a warning while executing the written code, we suggest you make some changes and re-execute it.

Here is an example:

Warning -- This may need more resources

With this, we have completed a brief explanation about errors and warnings in the C programming language.

As said before, even experienced programmers face errors while dealing with programming code. So, always make sure that you feel challenging whenever you see a programming error.

Before ending this book, here are some tips to improve your C programming skills exponentially:

1) Register yourself with GitHub and start reading various open-source code available. Good code can be written only when you are aware of the good code that has been written already.

2) Start contributing to open-source projects. Always start with simple projects and extend your skills by involving complex projects with a lot of contributors.

3) Don't feel low when you face errors. Clear your doubts with the help of forums such as Stack Overflow.

With this, we have completed a brief explanation about errors in this chapter and thus we are in the end parts of our book.

We have discussed a good number of topics related to C programming in this book.

All the best!

Conclusion

Glad that you have reached the end of this book. I hope you have enjoyed the content provided in the book as much we loved making this book.

What to do next?

As you have completed a complex and thorough book that deals with C programming it is now a huge test for you to apply your programming skills on real time projects. There are a lot of open-source projects that are waiting for a contribution. Remember that reading a lot of C language code will also help you understand the programming logics that C possesses.

That's it! Thanks for purchasing this book again and All the best!

www.ingramcontent.com/pod-product-compliance
Lightning Source LLC
La Vergne TN
LVHW051434050326
832903LV00030BD/3074